Seasons

by Brenda Power

Volume 1

Seasons

Literacy Leadership Wisdom *from* Choice Literacy

Choice Literacy, P.O. Box 790, Holden, Maine 04429
www.choiceliteracy.com

All original content was published in *The Big Fresh*®, the weekly newsletter of Choice Literacy.

Library of Congress Cataloging in Publication Data Pending

ISBN 978-1-60155-028-6

Cover and interior design by Martha Drury
Manufactured in the United States of America

16 15 14 13 11 10 9 8 7 6 5 4 3 2 1

Summer

Fall

Winter

Spring

Introduction

This collection of short readings for teachers and literacy leaders features excerpts from *The Big Fresh*, Choice Literacy's free weekly e-newsletter. In sorting through almost 200 brief essays, trying to decide what to include, I played with many different categories for organizing the book: community, collaboration, finding balance, taming assessments . . .

In the end, what struck me most in rereading more than three years' worth of issues was the rhythm of the year for educators. Our annual cycle is unlike that in any other profession—with the highs of the fall followed so quickly by the lows in winter, the quiet of summer planning contrasted with the rush of getting everything done in the spring.

For many subscribers to *The Big Fresh*, receiving the weekly email is a reminder to slow down. I hear from many subscribers about their routines of grabbing a cup of coffee or tea and taking a quiet moment to remember what matters most when working with students and colleagues. I love the emails I receive from readers every week, connecting my insights to theirs, gently chiding me if the advice is off, and most of all, sharing energy and optimism about colleagues, kids, and literacy learning.

The book is divided by seasons, with a reading for each week of the year—designed for flexible use in study groups, staff meetings, or just for reading and reflection on your own.

Teachers and literacy leaders have the best job in the world, even if some days it feels like the hardest job. I hope these readings help you sort through and make sense of it. It's a pleasure writing for you each week.

Brenda Power

Summer

Summer may be my favorite teaching season, if only because so many people think we have a three-month vacation. Many educators are on year-round contracts, but even those who are away from school during June, July, or August do much of their best work during this season. We immerse ourselves in the "re's"—reflecting, reconsidering, reorganizing, renewing. And when the summer goes well, we return to our classrooms re-energized for new challenges that await us.

A Chamber of Commerce Day

"We're having a Chamber of Commerce day here," Joan Moser told me on the phone a couple of days ago—and even though I'd never heard the phrase before, I knew exactly what she was talking about. We were 3,000 miles apart, but the weather in Maine (clear blue skies, low humidity, temperatures in the high 70s) was the same at her home in Tacoma, Washington. It's the sort of gorgeous day any community would use to advertise their town as the perfect place to live.

After I hung up the phone, I began to think about what a Chamber of Commerce day might look like for me professionally. I know it would include at least a little time talking with teachers about the newest books and activities they were trying in their classrooms. A really great day would have some time behind the cameras with the video crew, capturing some of those new practices. And it wouldn't be complete without cracking open some new office supply or piece of equipment, since I love trying out new tools.

We spend so much time talking about efficiency, productivity, and outcomes in schools . . . and too little time talking about what makes our work joyful. A clinical discussion of temperature, humidity, and cloud cover doesn't begin to capture how wonderful a perfect summer day can make you feel.

What does your perfect day look like in your school or classroom? Is it about books or breakthroughs with kids? Quiet reflection alone or great conversations with colleagues? Maybe all of the above? Most important: how can you get more of those moments in every day, and fewer of the ones that wear you down?

Making Dreams Come True

Years ago I forced myself to meet a financial planner, because I knew financial planning wasn't my strength. I saw the visit as similar to going to the dentist for a root canal—not a service I could perform myself, and certainly something I didn't look forward to. I told Jonathan the first time we met, "I'm not really sure why I'm here, because I love to work, so I can't ever imagine retiring." His reply: "Financial planning isn't really about retiring. It's about making your dreams come true."

Within five minutes of our first talk, I realized there was one dream financial planning could help my family achieve: getting a house on the water someday. Two years later, we bought our little dream house on the lake, where we live to this day. (Okay, it's lucky that the dream vision included a leaky roof, no garage, and no storage space . . . but we still marvel at our good fortune!)

Those first few minutes with the financial planner changed the way I view my work with teachers. Now when I first meet with teachers, I try to find a way to ask, "So how can I help make your dreams come true in your classroom?" Those may not be the exact words I use, but the impulse is always the same—to bring educators back to their hopes and dreams, and to build a partnership from there. Instead of seeing literacy leadership as helping children meet state standards or raising the quality of reading instruction in schools or coaching to raise achievement scores, what would happen if we defined our job as helping others make their professional dreams come true? None of us became teachers because we thought this job could make us rich. We teach because we started with inspiring visions of kids, books, and learning in classrooms, and saw ourselves in the thick of it.

Ask a teacher to explain her dream vision of working with children, or his ultimate goal in teaching reading and writing, and you've got a starting point for a truly fulfilling relationship with that teacher. In the end, everything else (from standards to high-quality teaching) can flow from that initial inspiration. If some colleagues view a visit from you with as much eagerness as a trip to the dentist or a fun-filled afternoon balancing the checkbook, then maybe "How can I help make your dreams come true in your classroom?" might be a way to begin to change the terms of your relationship.

A Place at the Table

When my parents moved to a smaller place years ago, they gave many of their furnishings to my siblings and me. I had only one request: I wanted the round oak table from the kitchen, the site of marathon card games, most family meals, and many happy memories from my childhood. My husband, daughter, and I drove 1,400 miles round-trip in the dog days of summer to pick up that table (with much grumbling en route), and traveled home with the U-Haul in tow.

We groaned and grunted as we carefully rolled the table into our own small house. But once it was in place, the house we had lived in for two years finally became a home. There is just something about the warm wood in that hundred-year-old table that gives a sense of stability, of comfort . . . that begs you to pull up a chair to chat or sort through a problem.

Nancie Atwell writes about the goal of having "dining-room table conversations" about books and writing in our classrooms. A few years ago Franki Sibberson realized there might be a literal truth in this ideal: if we bring real dining-room tables into our classrooms and converse at them, the whole tenor of the conversations might change. Franki added a wooden table and chairs to her classroom seating arrangement, and immediately saw the quality of talk in conferences and small groups lifted.

I'm sure there are good scientific reasons that could be teased out to explain why and how dining-room tables affect classroom talk. Here's my completely unscientific take. First, "coming to the table" promotes anticipation at home—of a meal, homework, shared tasks with people you love. Perhaps the background knowledge students bring to the task of "pulling up to the table" elevates their preparation a bit. Second, maybe a bunch of ultra-modern homes in Beverly Hills have dining-room furniture made of metal and plastic, but for the most part, cold metal and plastic tables are the norm only in schools—not anywhere else. Wood is just warmer—it shows its scars and history proudly. There's a sense of traditions being born and carried on when you're sitting at an old table, at a time when it seems like so little in our world endures.

If you want better conversations in your conferences with students, colleagues, or small groups this year, consider adding a "dining-room-style" table to your classroom or staff area. You can often find them at end-of-summer garage sales. You might be surprised at how quickly they can make your classroom feel more like home for students.

Reference
Atwell, Nancie. 1998. *In the Middle*. Portsmouth, NH: Heinemann.

The Beauty of Bare Walls

Years ago a good friend of mine took a teaching position in England. At the end of the summer, she went to the school to begin decorating her classroom before students arrived. Imagine her surprise when she discovered the school norm was no wall decorations at all to begin the year. Even the desks were heaped in the center of each classroom when the children entered. The idea was that students and teachers would create the room environment together, truly from scratch.

I don't know if this is the norm throughout England or the world, but my friend found it so powerfully effective in building community at the start of the school year that she continued the practice when she returned to the United States. It isn't easy to overcome cultural norms, and teaching norms can be especially ingrained, passed down from generation to generation. Taking pride in our wall displays, and spending a good chunk of late summer creating them, is one of those norms.

But before you cover every available foot of wall space with back-to-school finery, consider the lessons from brain researchers. We learn and retain information when it is anchored somehow in our experience. (We don't call all those big pieces of paper tacked up in the classroom meeting area "anchor charts" for nothing!) Starting with bare walls, and then building the content on the walls gradually through the class community's shared experiences, and especially through shared experiences with texts, almost guarantees that students will retain and refer to far more of the information on the classroom walls than the materials placed there by teachers in advance.

An easy principle to agree with, perhaps, but not so easy to put into practice if you have the Martha Stewart of Bulletin Boards gilding and hot-gluing her borders in the classroom next door at this very moment. To overcome the pressure to compete with colleagues, to swim against cultural norms, or even just to resist the urge to pick up a few more posters at the local teacher supply store requires a strong sense of purpose.

When I visited Max Brand's fifth-grade classroom in Dublin, Ohio, a few years ago, I was struck by all the colorful words, phrases, and drafts on the walls. I spent hours browsing the walls, and noticed students were continually adding to them, referring to them, or pointing out something on a wall during class discussions. Max described the walls as the class community's "Collective Writer's Notebook," and I loved the phrase. It set a standard for the walls, and gave students and Max some criteria for judging what should go on them, based on what was in their individual writer's notebooks.

What's your standard for your walls? How bare are you willing to go this August?

Breaking the Rules

What does it take to help others reach their full potential as learners and teachers?

What do you need to reach your own potential?

If you're a literacy leader, you need expertise not just in how children learn to read and write, but in how people change. And if that isn't complicated enough, you've also got to make sure you get your own needs met as a learner. Late summer is the time when many of us are looking at our roles and responsibilities with new eyes, if only because we've had a little time off over the past few months to do some reflecting and set goals for the year.

If you're assessing your relationships with colleagues and how you might improve them, you may find this list of questions from Marcus Buckingham and Curt Coffman about work environments helpful. Buckingham and Coffman are the authors of the book *First, Break All the Rules: What the World's Greatest Managers Do Differently*. I'm not crazy about the word managers—it conjures up a vision of row upon row of white cubicles. Yet I find that their checklist provides good benchmarks for thinking through what people need to feel valued and thrive in any work environment.

Ask yourself the questions, and then imagine how your colleagues might respond:

1. Do I know what is expected of me at work?
2. Do I have the materials and equipment I need to do my work right?
3. At work, do I have the opportunity to do what I do best every day?
4. In the last seven days, have I received recognition or praise for good work?
5. Does my supervisor, or someone at work, seem to care about me as a person?
6. Is there someone at work who encourages my development?
7. At work, do my opinions seem to count?
8. Does the mission/purpose of my company make me feel like my work is important?
9. Are my co-workers committed to doing quality work?
10. Do I have a best friend at work?
11. In the last six months, have I talked with someone about my progress?
12. At work, have I had the opportunities to learn and grow?

If you're able to answer yes to all these questions, there's no doubt you're working in an amazing school. And if there are concerns about your school environment you haven't been able to name, the questions may give you and your colleagues an entry point for identifying problems and starting to tackle them.

Reference

Buckingham, Marcus, and Curt Coffman. 1999. *First, Break All the Rules: What the World's Greatest Managers Do Differently.* New York: Simon and Schuster.

Small Acts of Liberation

Today I was reading Elizabeth Berg's new collection of short stories, *The Day I Ate Whatever I Wanted and Other Small Acts of Liberation.* In the lead story, the main character gets upset when two trim women show up at her morning Weight Watchers meeting, so she goes on an all-day eating adventure. At one point, as she is ranting about food and points and deprivation, she makes this declaration:

> *If you're one of those people who doesn't [ever deprive yourself], stop right here, you are not invited to the rest of this story.*

I gasped and laughed at these words. You just don't do this in fiction. Characters shouldn't suddenly start talking to readers, and they certainly aren't allowed to uninvite all the skinny ones from finishing the rest of the story. Berg broke one of the most important rules in fiction writing, and when she did, I went from being charmed by this character to falling in love with her.

I was thinking of rules earlier this week when a close friend phoned. She is thinking of starting her own business, and asked for some advice. A career change will be a good move for her, and it was one of those conversations where I wanted to say something to let her know I thought she was making a wise and wonderful decision, even though I know little about the business she is launching. I found myself telling her about something I did when I started Choice

Literacy: I dipped into savings that I promised myself years ago I would never touch. It was the biggest personal financial rule I'd ever broken, and in retrospect it made all the difference for success the first year. "I'm not suggesting you do the same thing," I told her. "It might be a terrible mistake for you. But there's probably a big rule you're carrying around inside you, a sacred one, that you'll likely need to break if you want to rewrite your life by launching this business."

When you think about it, most of our time is spent either following the rules or trying to do a better job following the rules (whatever they are at that moment, in that particular situation). And our families and communities depend upon us living this way. We curse the idiot cruising down the breakdown lane on the hottest day of the summer while the rest of us are stopped and steaming in construction traffic. We stew about the jerk who shows up to the staff meeting a half hour late and then spends the rest of it answering email on his laptop. We lost patience long ago with the princess three classroom doors down who can't be bothered to turn in her assessment data on the day it's due in the fall like the rest of us.

There's no civility, graciousness, or enjoyment of daily routines without some principles to guide us. We search for the right words and the right lessons to give at the right time so students will learn more. And out there somewhere is the perfect protocol—the right structure delivered with just the right tone so our grade-level team discussions can flourish.

Amidst all those collective rules, we've got our own personal codes. Some are so important that they can't be scrawled on scraps of paper we tuck away in our minds. . . . These are ones we've chiseled in stone, carrying the weight of them everywhere, just to remind ourselves of how much they represent who we are and what we believe.

And yet . . . breaking the right rule at the right time in the right way makes all the difference in overcoming a personal or professional logjam. When a rule is broken that needs to be broken, we dazzle ourselves, amazed at how much more is possible without that arbitrary edict that has been blocking us.

If you're stuck on a project or in a professional situation, there is likely a rule you need to break. The more stuck you are, the more likely it's a stone tablet rule, not a paper rule. I can't begin to guess what the rule is for you, because we've all carved out different codes to get us through our days. I'm guessing it wouldn't be a rule that would cause your spouse to leave you or the IRS to audit you or your principal to fire you on the spot. Beyond that, it could be almost anything. If you're a literacy leader, some days your biggest responsibility will be giving a colleague permission to break a rule. Not just any rule, but the one rule that for that person, in that situation, could make all the difference in solving the problem vexing them.

Reference

Berg, Elizabeth. 2008. *The Day I Ate Whatever I Wanted and Other Small Acts of Liberation.* New York: Random House.

Pretzels and Purple Cows

I entered the gate area of the airport at 9 PM on a hot July night and saw dozens of people sprawled over seats and on the floor—teens napping with their heads at awkward angles on backpacks, babies fussing, an elderly couple holding hands. I glanced at the empty counter of that Midwest-based airline and saw a brief note explaining that the flight these folks were waiting for was delayed eight hours (with a few hours of waiting still ahead for them).

By my calculation, the stranded passengers were in stage 3 of the four stages of flight delay grief. Long past irritation (stage 1), or scrambling to change connections and arrival plans (stage 2), they had that look of bleached exhaustion that comes only after many hours of breathing stale air in an airport terminal. (If you've ever traveled and been delayed, you may have experienced stage 4, acceptance: you may get home, you may not, but you've acknowledged that it's completely out of your control.)

Luckily the JetBlue flight at a nearby gate was on schedule, and within a few minutes a JetBlue gate agent arrived to begin checking in passengers. She took one look at the full gate area, glanced at the other counter with its notice about the long delay, and disappeared through a door. Within a minute she came out with a crate holding bottles of water. She set it on the empty counter of the other airline. Went back for another crate of water. Went back one last time for a large box of snack crackers and cookies. She then announced, "I see a lot of people here have been waiting a long time for a delayed flight. I thought you might enjoy some water and a snack. Please help yourselves." She then proceeded to start checking in people for the JetBlue flight.

I was amazed. Most airlines because of relentless budget cutting have even stopped giving out the tiny in-flight bags of pretzels that used to be ubiquitous on airplanes. (Those little bags of pretzels cost all of two cents each, so eliminating them takes the phrase *nickel and diming* to a whole new level.) I'd never seen any airline provide water and snacks to people in a gate area who were delayed. Yet this gate agent went beyond that, providing refreshments to customers from another airline. The city the stranded passengers were flying to isn't even served by JetBlue, so what would be the point in trying to win them over?

Seth Godin is an entrepreneur who has written about the concept of "the purple cow" in business. Simply explained, if you're driving through the countryside, you might be surprised and delighted to notice a cow grazing in the field. But once you see dozens of cows, you won't notice them anymore. What would it take to get your attention? A purple cow—something so truly out of the ordinary that you'd have to stop, get out of the car, and wonder how in the world it came to be.

That brief period in the gate area was a "purple cow" experience for me. It made me wonder what kind of management was in place that allowed the gate agent to act on a kind impulse instantly, without worrying that she would be reprimanded (or fired!) for giving away $42 worth of snacks. And this at a time when most airlines were begrudging their own passengers two cents' worth of pretzels. It made me realize that most "purple cow acts" never happen, because there is no time for a cost-benefits analysis or to get approval from three layers of management. Even if you did the analysis and went through an approval process, you couldn't immediately calculate the value of the act.

Can your school be a purple cow? Of course it can, but it takes a level of empowering colleagues that is going to lead to grief now and again. People will have wonderful ideas for small kindnesses and exceptional acts that can't possibly move through the approval process quickly enough, will irritate the wrong people, and will cost money when dollars couldn't be scarcer. Yet in the end, those acts that matter—being kind and generous when it isn't easy and certainly isn't expected—are what stay in the memory far longer than the ordinary miracles we expect from teachers every day.

Perhaps one day next month or next year, when a bunch of parents are hanging out at a barbecue, complaining about high taxes and lousy schools, someone who has seen a purple cow will interrupt the group and say, "That may be true for you. But they do the most extraordinary thing at my daughter's school . . ." or "My son's teacher isn't like that—you're not going to believe what she did for us last spring. . . ." Purple cows lodge in your head, and you can't help but share them with others.

For example, this JetBlue story was shared with tens of thousands of people who read this newsletter, written by someone who doesn't work for JetBlue (and doesn't know anyone who does). I'm thinking publicity like this was probably worth the $42 of refreshments that gate agent set out. That's probably the entire point of purple cow moments: there is no sense that they will lead to great publicity or material gain. They are just remarkable, unexpected acts that build their own buzz.

Reference
Godin, Seth. 2009. *Purple Cow*. New York: Portfolio.

Pechu-Kucha

When forced to work within a strict framework the imagination is taxed to its utmost—and will produce its richest ideas. Given total freedom the work is likely to sprawl.

T. S. Eliot

When I was a college professor, I had colleagues who set aside their entire summer to write, since we were all under "publish or perish" pressure. They didn't write anything during the fall and spring semesters, saving their energy for the long writing days in July.

Over the years, I realized these folks were the least likely to produce any publications. The people who published were the ones who set aside a little time every day, even just 10 or 15 minutes, to peck away at projects. That daily time didn't stop them from taking whole days or weeks to write, too—but the daily discipline was what led to long-term writing success for most of us.

I wonder why so many of us produce the most when we have the least amount of time. I've been reading this week about *pecha-kucha,* a presentation format developed in Tokyo by Mark Dytham and Astrid Klein. Pecha-kucha presentations include 20 slides, each shown for 20 seconds—no more, no less. The commentary must be in sync with the visuals. You have 6 minutes, 40 seconds to tell your story or pitch your product or ignite the room with your revolutionary idea.

Pecha-kucha has a cult following around the globe, with Pecha-Kucha Nights popular in more than 80 countries. Adherents present their latest creations in hip multimedia venues (it sounds like karaoke for those who love PowerPoint). Garr Reynolds writes about it in his book *Presentation Zen*:

> *If nothing else, the pecha-kucha method is good training and good practice. Everyone should try pecha-kucha; it's a good exercise for getting your story down even if you do not use the method exactly for your live talk. It doesn't matter whether or not you can implement the pecha-kucha "20X20 6:40" method exactly in your company or school, but the spirit behind it and the concept of "restrictions as liberators" can be applied to most any presentation situation.*
>
> *(41)*

I haven't tried pecha-kucha, but I love the idea of forcing big ideas and massive projects into tiny spaces. If you are one of the lucky educators who have long stretches of time this summer to work on looming professional tasks, it's tempting to slot whole weeks for tackling them. And it's just that sprawl that may have you coming up empty when it comes to getting much accomplished.

What if you tried a different approach this year? Pretend your days in July and early August are jam-packed with teaching chores (in others words, imagine it's a typical March or April stretch). You've got only 23 minutes each morning to work on that big project. Why 23 minutes? Because it's my lucky number. Seriously, pick a number that is small and just that arbitrary—17, 19, 34. Set a timer, work those minutes on the big project, and then get on with your day.

A daily tight framework doesn't preclude taking a full day or week to get the job done, but it does free you up from the lack of focus or direction (or insistent pull of procrastination) that comes from so much unstructured time.

Reference

Reynolds, Garr. 2008. *Presentation Zen*. Berkeley, CA: New Riders Press.

Look Up

Today after the electrician leaves, our kitchen remodel will finally be finished. I never really appreciated my kitchen sink until it was gone . . . for a month. Now that the kitchen is complete, I realize the worst of the clutter was near the ceiling.

There was a one-foot gap between the top of our old cupboards and the ceiling. I thought it was the perfect place to store vases and serving platters and all manner of rarely used junk. But now that this space is cleared, I realize what an eyesore it was.

It's funny how our vision works once we get accustomed to a living area. When we enter our classrooms, when it comes to noticing clutter, we tend to look at table or floor levels—jumbles of books, papers, or coats may grab our attention. But when others first enter our rooms, they take in the whole of it, from the lights above on down to the floors, and their eyes are often drawn to those messes high up that we may no longer notice.

I remember years ago entering a colleague's large office. She prided herself on the homey touches in it: always fresh flowers on the conferring table, neat bookshelves, and scented candles. We were chatting away when I asked, "Hey, what's in the orange boxes?" On her highest shelf in a far corner were more than a dozen large orange file organizers—that telltale ugly orange shade that usually signals some sort of reading program.

She pursed her lips and replied, "You know, I don't really know. They were there when Charlie Hargood had the office six years ago. They are so high up, I can't reach them, and I just forgot they were there." The next time I visited, I noticed the boxes were gone—a janitor had pulled them down for her, and they discovered an obsolete phonics program that went straight into the trash bin.

If you're reorganizing your classroom or staff work areas, don't forget to look up. We're often delighted when we "discover" a little space on top of a coat closet or high shelves that can be used to store the materials we rarely use. Since the materials are out of the way, we don't have to worry about children or ourselves tripping over them, and they are often an odd jumble. The truth is that clutter near the top of the room weighs the whole environment down, and getting rid of it can lighten and open up the room immediately. If what you're saving is rarely used, it can likely be placed in a storage cabinet or even the garage till needed. And chances are, much of it likely could be recycled or discarded anyway. If you needed it, you'd have it in a place where it was easier to reach.

Learners Permitted

My 15-year-old daughter started driver's education last month, which means that driving with her over the past few weeks has been a special kind of hell for me. Dee hasn't had enough training to get her learner's permit, but she has acquired enough skills and knowledge to critique my driving . . . oh, pretty much every time I make a turn or pull up to a stoplight. Which would be every two to three minutes. Without fail.

The experience has made me think a lot about the role of any coach, and especially literacy coaches in classrooms. What I've realized all over again is this:

- No one likes to be coached by someone who doesn't have skills or experience with the activity being coached. Everything always looks easier from the outside.

- We can all benefit from the perspective of someone watching our moves closely. I am a much better driver this month than I was last month, just because some of my sloppiest habits have been pointed out to me. Repeatedly.

- We work hardest at the things we care most about. Since Dee finally got her permit a few days ago, I have been amazed by how careful and smart she is in her driving. She eagerly seeks feedback after every drive, asks questions throughout the process, and is open to the honest analysis of her skills.

Most of all, I have been reminded that those of us who coach others really need the experience periodically of learning something new, preferably something that is a true challenge. What are you planning to learn this summer? Who will be your coach? I will be in film school for a week. I go almost every year, and it's always exhausting and exciting. I'm not particularly skilled with equipment or technology, and the lingo of filmmaking is foreign to me. Yet I always come away with a new perspective on art and learning, and a few practical tools for our video work here at Choice Literacy.

The Unwowables

When we finished presenting at some workshops last summer, "The Sisters" (Joan Moser and Gail Boushey) and I had an extra evening together. We decided to celebrate by treating ourselves to a spectacular dinner out.

The restaurant we visited wasn't just any old café—it's a small place on the Maine coast that has been visited by reviewers from the *New York Times* and *Gourmet* magazine over the years, with everyone from top national publications to the folks writing at foodie websites giving it rapturous reviews. Walking up the steps to the charming building was like entering a fairyland by way of a bistro, with tiny twinkle lights and the kind of details that let you know someone put a lot of care into creating the perfect dining environment.

It was Monday, a quiet night, and the early crowd was just us and one other table of people who arrived a few minutes later. Joan, Gail, and I were tucking into the second course of our five-course lobster-tasting menu, but the other diners next to us hadn't seemed to have made up their minds about their order. Finally, a man from their table motioned the server over. "We're leaving," he announced. "Just give us a check for these drinks." The server assured him she would send it right over, and then asked why they weren't staying for dinner. He glanced around, waving his hands as he proclaimed loudly, "This place, this menu—it just didn't WOW us."

"It just didn't wow him? It just didn't WOW him?!" I whispered loudly to Joan and Gail as they shushed me. Now, granted, we are country gals, and not long ago "upscale dining" for us was any restaurant that didn't include a "with cheese" option for all the entrees. Even so, it was hard to believe anyone wouldn't think this restaurant had the wow factor down, from the unique entrees to the warm and trendy decor.

I've thought about it since, and came up with three possibilities for why that guy wasn't wowed:

1. He takes pride in never being wowed. I've come across people like him in professional settings, and they are never impressed. Their identity is wrapped up in having higher, better standards than everyone they work with. In my experience, these people are deeply insecure about their own work performance, often with good reason.
2. He wanted something that wasn't on the menu. It might have been a two-pound steak, or a kumquat—who knows? But when the item wasn't there, his needs and wants weren't met, so he walked away.
3. He couldn't afford the prices. It was a lovely but very expensive restaurant, and "not being wowed" was a way to save face.

You might be hard at work right now on a project, presentation, or classroom display that you are sure will wow everyone. Part of why we spend so many more hours than we should on our work is that we anticipate that moment when faces will light up and everyone will be amazed by what we've done. Just remember there is always that one person who will not be wowed, will likely never be wowed, and has the ability to send you trudging back to your car at the end of the day completely deflated. When that happens to me, too often I spend the drive home worrying and obsessing over that one person who said, "Meh, I've seen better" instead of celebrating the dozens or hundreds who loved the effort.

The server's attitude was just right. She asked for feedback, thanked the group for stopping in, then quickly prepared the table for the next diners. She never missed a beat, throughout the evening answering all our questions and delivering every course with flair and good humor.

Don't worry about the unwowables. It may be insecurity that keeps them from acknowledging the quality of your work, or a fear that they will be held to the same standard, or even their need to claim allegiance to the one program or curricular idea that fuels their own teaching and learning. At some level you're a threat, and their response isn't about the work at all.

Of course, it's easy for me to write these words, since I don't have a boss or colleague I have to deal with every day who is unwowable. But it's still good advice, because if you're a person who routinely produces incredible work, the unwowables can grind you down and keep you from doing your best. And that's a loss for everyone else in your community who appreciates your efforts.

In the year since that dining experience, Joan, Gail, and I have enjoyed our new catchphrase often when we're together. Whenever we read a spectacular book or walk into a gorgeous classroom or view a particularly thoughtful lesson together, one of us is likely to wrinkle her nose and whisper, "It just didn't WOW me." Then we all cackle like idiots. It's our code for highlighting and enjoying beautiful work—and reminding ourselves of all those "wows" in our midst and what fun it is to share them with others.

Mirrors and Models

Do you ever wonder why people get hooked on the Summer Olympics, watching sports they probably won't think about for another four years? In 2008 my favorite athlete was gymnast Shawn Johnson from Iowa, so graceful in defeat for many days. A world champion before the events began, she was tagged to be the gal who came home with a fistful of gold medals and ended up on a box of Wheaties. But beginning with teammates' stumbles in the first days of competition, through a repeat again and again of slightly low scores from judges, she never cried. Shawn always praised her teammates, enjoyed their successes, and said she was thankful for the trio of silver medals around her neck. And when she finally, on her very last routine of the competition, nailed her flips and whirls on the impossibly narrow balance beam and landed her only gold medal, it was one of those transcendent moments that reminds me why the Olympics are so addictive.

Scientists have recently been decoding how "mirror neurons" in our brains work. They've realized that humans are wired to connect with others, to live vicariously through others' experiences, in much stronger ways than we once thought. Your brain doesn't differentiate much between watching someone do something and doing it yourself—which is why there are so many obsessed sports fans in the world. Most important for teachers, these mirror neurons are also a key to how we learn. Just watching someone read a book teaches us more than we ever realized about the reading process. And we use our emotions to readily connect those experiences to other related tasks (either physically or emotionally). I will never be a gymnast (beyond the contortions I go through to get through airport security screening). But I can connect to the feeling of almost, not quite reaching a goal again and again, and finally succeeding. What teacher hasn't experienced weeks or months of helping a struggling student almost, but not quite, grasp a concept? It makes those breakthrough moments all the more sweet.

Mirror neurons are also the reason modeling in classrooms is so essential. When students see the strategies teachers use to tackle difficult texts, no matter the genre, their brains don't differentiate between their experiences and ours. The teacher's strategies become part of the mix that fires up whenever a student approaches a new text. Likewise, all those whole-class activities to build community around reading and writing early in the year become ingredients in the chemical soup in our students' brains as they read and write on their own. The consequences of broken mirror neurons can also be dire, as any teacher who has worked with an autistic child knows.

What about mirror neurons in staff settings? Simply put, our moms were right: we shouldn't hang out with the wrong crowd, and we need to choose our role models carefully. Mirror neurons imitate and absorb what they see around us whether we like what we're seeing or not. If you're surrounded by negative, unhappy people, it's human nature that you're going to absorb that outlook over time. Sometimes toxic environments or people can't be avoided, but it's important to note that when it comes to "emotional contagions," negative environments have more powerful effects than positive ones. If you have colleagues who are always resentful or angry, you owe it to yourself and your students to limit your time with them. If you have to spend time with them, even decreasing eye contact or verbal interactions can help limit what your brain's mirror neurons pick up.

Beyond the emotional benefits, there is another reason literacy leaders will benefit from hanging out with optimistic folks: it makes you a better problem solver, since happiness is associated with a higher-functioning left side of the brain (the logical, problem-solving area).

Shawn Johnson spent years training physically for the Olympics. But it may be her mind and heart that were most carefully honed for success. By staying positive and embracing the achievements of others, she eventually reached her goal. And thanks to mirror neurons, many teachers around the world have a tiny bit of Shawn's positive chemical rush tucked away in our brains, too, as we face all the unique challenges a new school year brings.

Hopscotch Kid in a Jump-Rope World

What I remember most about elementary school is that there were just too darn many of us kids. At the height of the baby boom in our little town, with no money for a new school, everyone just made do. In third grade, desks were scrunched together so tightly, there was no room to walk down aisles. Kids were dangling off of old heating radiators and on window ledges, and lunch was served in four shifts.

Before my fourth-grade year, they un-condemned an old schoolhouse the town owned that hadn't been used in 20 years and bused the fourth graders there. By "un-condemned," I don't mean the community tidied it up by doing little things like removing the asbestos or anything that would actually make it livable; they just reopened the doors and hoped for the best. There were many no-water days with portable toilets when the well wasn't working right, and parents knew to pack extra sweaters all winter long because the furnace was unreliable. But when you're nine, everything feels like an adventure, and boarding those extra buses that carried us fourth graders away from the big elementary school off to our little hovel in the woods made us feel special.

The next year someone ruined all the fun (most likely the state health inspector or Centers for Disease Control) by condemning that old school again, and for good. Drastic measures were needed, so the town council begged adjourning communities to peel off a few kids from locations closest to their schools. Maps were redrawn, and I found myself in the unexpected role of being a new kid in fifth grade at a little school in the next town over. The first day of recess was disastrous. I had my chalk in hand, ready to make friends over hopscotch. No one else was carrying chalk. Ropes unspooled all around me, and within moments elaborate games of jump rope were unfolding all over the concrete play area, with singsong chants echoing through the air.

We'd never played jump rope at my old school; jacks was my fallback game. I didn't have a clue how this style of jump rope was played—those were some fancy chants and jumps. By day two of school, a perfect sunny September afternoon, I was sitting on a bench, reading a book, determined to pretend I'd prefer to read rather than play all year long.

It was then that my fifth-grade teacher, Mrs. Thompson, approached me. She was nearly 60 years old, 4 foot 10, had a shock of short red hair and thick glasses, and weighed maybe 90 pounds soaking wet. She was given to breaking out in show tunes and dancing in class when the math textbook got boring. At any moment, those eagle Coke-bottle eyes might also intercept a love note passed up the aisle, and she would stop whatever she was doing and have the person holding the note stand up to read it aloud. Everyone adored her and was scared spitless by her at the same time. She ran a very tight cruise ship.

"Tell me, did you read books at recess at your old school?" she asked.

"No, I usually played hopscotch," I replied. "But I like reading."

"Well, there's no reading allowed at recess here," she said briskly. "Give me the book." She snapped her fingers, and her hand shot out to take it from me.

No reading at recess? I was appalled, scrambling to come up with a way to fill all those noon hours all year long. Not to mention this was a school, so a rule against reading sounded a little fishy. I did something I rarely did as the shyest kid in the class: I spoke up. "Why?" I challenged.

Mrs. Thompson wasn't used to being questioned, so she stammered a bit. "Because . . . because . . . because the sun damages the books. And then we'd have no books, and if we've got no books, we've got no school." Now, that made perfect sense, so I handed the book over. She then grabbed my hand. "Have you ever tried jump rope?" she asked as she pulled me off the bench. I shook my head, and my stomach dropped at what would come next. She would introduce me to the girls playing nearby and tell them to include me, and they would welcome me in the classic fifth-grade girls' style after Mrs. Thompson left— like a rump roast thrown to a pack of hyenas.

Yet she did something totally unexpected, a quality that had already made her my all-time favorite teacher—she was always doing something totally unexpected. "Girls, slow down the ropes. I'm coming in," Mrs. Thompson bellowed. "And I'm bringing a friend." Moments later, somehow, some way, I found myself in the center of the rope, holding hands, facing Mrs. Thompson, fervently doing my best to keep the beat. She stayed only a minute or so, then jumped out and went on her way to terrorize and dazzle her next victim on the edges of the playground.

I won't lie and say fifth grade was easy from then on, and I breathed a sigh of relief the next year when I was back with all my old friends for sixth grade, crammed into yet another too-small junior high school. But Mrs. Thompson forced me to literally jump right in and start making new friends.

So who's the hopscotch kid in a jump-rope world this year at your school? A new teacher or two or three? A couple of big new immigrant families? A curriculum coordinator poached from the next district over? Most school cultures have it ingrained that those hopscotch kids have to prove themselves to us—learn our rules, and play our games. And it's terrifying when you're the new kid (even if you're a new kid pushing 50) and don't even know where to begin. It doesn't matter if you've got a great new teacher orientation day planned in a few weeks, or mentors assigned, or a potluck on the books in October for new families. Now is the time to pick up the phone and take the newbie out to lunch, or pop over with some school supplies and a gift card to the local coffee shop for a quick cup of tea and sympathy. If you reach out now, you will have their gratitude forever, and everyone will have a little less stress and awkwardness during those first busy days of school.

My last phone call to Mrs. Thompson was during a trip home from college, when I was 20. She was dying of cancer, and wouldn't take visitors because she "looked so awful." She had prided herself on her trim suits and accessories. In our little burg, she was quite the fashion plate, so I know the chemo and being bedridden must have been a terrible indignity. I was awkward, and told her I understood. I wish now I had told her she would always be beautiful to me—because she is. Frozen in time, that too-red head thrown back, bumping against a vivid September sky as she kept time, laughing and exclaiming, "Isn't this the most fun?!"

Fall

It's a sign of our optimism that everything feels new in the fall, even if we've been teaching 30 years. The air is crisp, the scent of the classroom is clean, and we're even determined that this will be the year we get along with that harridan running the classroom next door.

Of course, it can all fall apart pretty quickly—that crisp air becomes cold, the more exotic scents of children overwhelm the hardiest air fresheners in our classrooms, and best not to mention how soon we revert to polite silences with difficult colleagues. Even with all that, fall is still a wonder, brimming with possibilities for us year after year.

A Different View of September

Last year in early September I found myself sitting with friends in a park. It was late afternoon, the sky was a brilliant blue, and we noticed the first red leaves in the large oak trees around us. I was just thinking the day couldn't be more perfect when one of my friends remarked, "September is such a sad time of year, isn't it?" Everyone agreed quickly, speaking of melancholy and shorter days and despair at the end of summer.

I was so stunned I didn't say anything. This is my favorite time of year. I realized I was the only educator in the group, which is why my perspective was so different from theirs. I love September for all the reasons many of you do. What other profession gets a fresh start every year, the chance to begin again with rearranged furniture, new plans, new faces? Something about that crisp air calls for truces even with the colleagues we disagree with the most (not that the comity necessarily lasts beyond the leaves falling).

There is a spirit of possibility I savor, a delight in getting back into rhythms and routines—and creating a few new ones based on what I've learned over the summer. Of the many gifts we have in this profession, a view of September that is different from the rest of the world's may be one of the best and least acknowledged.

Impulse Buys

Quick quiz: What foods are the most common impulse buys in large supermarkets, with customers buying far more of the goods than they consume?

If you guessed potato chips, cookies, or some other junk, you might be surprised. People are most likely to buy fruits and vegetables on impulse, driven by the urge to eat more healthful meals. Unfortunately, a fair amount of those veggies rot before they are eaten. Retailers capitalize on this urge, arranging the layout of most grocery stores to ensure that customers walk through the produce section first, while their carts are still almost empty.

There's a science to the layout of grocery stores that teachers and literacy leaders can learn from as they think about children and community members walking through their building and classrooms. What's the traffic pattern for people entering your school? Where do they linger? And most important, do you give them anything to pick up and read on "impulse" in these valuable spaces?

For example, how about a wish list of books needed for classroom libraries? Parents may want to clean out those home libraries of Harry Potter and Magic Treehouse books this time of year if their children have outgrown them, and they can get a tax credit for a charitable deduction at the same time. How about some copies of a one-page article on tips for read-alouds at home, with a sign encouraging anyone to take a copy?

Although bulletin boards with notices on them are terrific, including business cards with the information to carry away (like a brief "Important Dates" card with parent conference, literacy nights, and inservice dates) gives parents something to post on the fridge and refer to later. In classrooms, a display of "Our Favorite New Books" near the door for parents to browse, with notes from students about why they are favorites, gives family members something worth lingering over. Parents want to know more and do more to help the young readers and writers in their lives, but there is never enough time. Thinking through traffic patterns and waiting areas in your school and classroom allows you to capitalize on the impulse family members have to learn more and do more in those moments we all spend waiting and wandering through schools.

What Will You Learn This Year?

If we resist our passions, it is more through their weakness than from our strength.

Francois de la Rochefoucauld

When I was working with young teachers, I had a trick for discovering which ones really didn't enjoy reading. I'd ask what book they were looking forward to reading in their free time. I'd always have a student or two who replied that they didn't have much time to read for fun but hoped one day to read more of the classics from authors like Shakespeare or Tolstoy. Maybe it was a response they thought I wanted to hear, and in a way, it was. It made me realize they'd probably never developed the habit of reading for pleasure, or the confidence in their choices (no matter how trashy or low-brow). I then had a goal of helping them to discover their literary tastes and find at least one book (any book at all) that they would truly love.

What are you most looking forward to learning about this year in your classroom? Do you reject the first idea that pops into your head and settle for something else? It can be hard for teachers to embrace their passions as readers, writers, and learners. Too often we dismiss the thing we really want to study or think about, because we studied it last year. And the year before. And it's not one of the mandates from the district office. And it doesn't seem deep enough, or trendy enough, or sophisticated in any way.

The truth is it can take years, sometimes a lifetime, to puzzle through even one aspect of learning to read and write. Following that passion can energize your teaching and elevate your mood the whole year long.

So what do you want to learn about this year? And what do you really want to read next? I hope you give yourself permission to embrace those passions this fall and throughout the school year.

Like Falling in Love

In 1983, English professor Peter Biedler said, "We've got to get our students to the point where they stop asking, 'Will this be on the test?' and start asking, 'Will this be like falling in love?'" When I was first learning how to teach, in the early 1980s, I wrote that quote on an index card and put it next to my state-of-the-art Selectric typewriter. I thought there was too much testing in the schools I was visiting, and I wanted to remind myself daily of what was most important in setting up an evaluation system in my own classroom someday. Seems quaint, doesn't it?

Through the years, I stubbornly kept that quote next to my first word processor, my first desktop computer, my first laptop. Today there is more testing than ever larded into the school year, but the quote still resonates for me. When the whole world says otherwise, we have to remind ourselves—through the observations we make, the stories we share with parents and colleagues, the records we choose to keep with students—that success in literacy really isn't all about acing the test. Finding a new favorite author, speaking out for the first time in a class discussion, taking a risk by trying a new genre in writing . . . These are the events that matter most to those of us who love literacy and want to inspire that passion in others. And somehow, we've got to find ways to include those moments in the evaluations we share with parents and students.

Inviting or Overwhelming?

Have you ever attended a social gathering where you knew almost no one, but everyone else seemed to know each other well? I remember almost a year ago attending a community potluck hosted by a service organization I admire. It was a cold October night, and I can still recall my nerves as I walked up to the front door, snow crunching under my feet, clutching a plate of homemade shortbread. Once the door flew open and someone grabbed my coat, I was enveloped in light, noise, and the sights and sounds of more than a hundred people mingling, laughing, and crowding together in the large space.

I felt totally overwhelmed. I had a fierce urge to step quickly back out the door into the calm quiet of the night, even though that meant I would have to leave my coat behind. It seemed a small price to pay for getting away from all those people.

But I didn't really have that option, because within moments a kind older woman grasped my hand with a firm shake and started taking me around the room, introducing me to some of her friends. Once she'd left 20 minutes later, I sat down in one of the half dozen or so areas of the room arranged with couches and chairs, and immediately was invited into a conversation about an environmental project the group was taking on.

I think back on that event, and I know many of the things that stressed me out at the start probably were counted as pluses by the event organizers: the large turnout, the open format, the absence of any agenda. In classrooms, some of the things we highlight as positives early in the year in building our classroom communities can overwhelm the more shy or socially awkward students.

Human nature does have some built-in mechanisms for welcoming new members into communities. Anthropologists talk about the "stranger handler" in any culture; someone in any environment will designate herself as the person to greet new people and give them an informal tour. Look up when someone new enters your classroom during an unstructured time, and you'll immediately see who your stranger handler is—the child who takes it upon herself to walk right up and start making the new person comfortable.

But it takes more than a good stranger handler to build a classroom community around literacy. Students who struggle with reading can be overwhelmed or discouraged by the hundreds of books we've arranged so carefully in bins and on shelves. We see all these colorful texts and displays as inviting; they may see it as far too much to take in and absorb all at once. We provide less structured times to allow students to connect and make independent choices for reading . . . but for some students, it's still too much noise, light, and crowds.

Heading into late September is always a good time to take the pulse of your classroom community. Who is the stranger handler? Who is thriving? Who is overwhelmed by the choices of books and literacy activities?

Bubbles and Books

The problem isn't that I'm a good teacher, or even a terrible teacher. The problem is some days I appear to be a twit who's been let loose among children.

Sylvia Ashton Warner

It was almost the end of a successful day of substitute teaching in first grade early in my career. At least it was "successful" as I defined it in those harrowing days of being let loose among children, with little training and some days even less common sense. There had been no blood, no tears, no outright anarchy among the seven-year-olds. I hadn't raised my voice once, though I had blinked the lights so many times throughout the day to get their attention that a few kids were still seeing stars.

Maybe I was feeling a bit cocky, or maybe I was just too tired to think straight. But in the rug area after the 2:30 PM read-aloud, I had an inspiration. "Boys and girls, it's been such a great day, and I can't wait to give Mrs. McLure a wonderful report about your behavior and learning. You know what would make the day perfect? Let's leave the room even cleaner than we found it. Let's all tidy up the classroom before the bell rings in 15 minutes and you need to go home."

The room was a disaster, with piles of yarn and paints from the morning art project still out, books and crayons scattered across desks, and even a lone green sock hanging off the edge of the rocking chair. I figured I might save myself 30 minutes of cleaning after school by enlisting the kids to help. Everyone whooped enthusiastically and started scurrying around, emptying wastebaskets and picking up stray bits of paper on the floor.

A few minutes later I ran to the back of the room to take care of an emergency involving a rumble by the classroom bathroom, some water, and many, many soap bubbles. I mopped, scolded, cajoled, and finally returned to the classroom library area just as the bell for the end of the day was ringing.

There, dumped in the middle of the rug, were books. Hundreds and hundreds of books—every basket and shelf emptied from the classroom library. A tow-headed sprite explained, "We're sorting all the books by color. It'll be way neater than before." There was one small basket of books, all red, sitting lonely on the shelf . . . which was as far as they had gotten in their execution of the plan.

A blur of backpacks, lunch boxes, hugs good-bye . . . and minutes later every child was gone. I sat in the middle of the classroom for a quiet moment, wondering yet again if brain surgeons or beauticians ever had days like these. Then I rolled up my sleeves and spent the next four hours rearranging the classroom library back into some semblance of order. It was full dark outside by the time I finally left the school with the custodian.

Of the many humbling experiences I've had working with children over the years, this was one of the most instructive. First, I never again completely turned my back on a soap dispenser in a classroom when I was in charge. Second, I realized yet again that children have very different ways of sorting and organizing information than we do. It's no wonder we spend so much time helping students understand genre and text features and styles and their own quirks as readers. There are so many ways to sort through books to find what you want or need to read, but they aren't readily apparent when you're six . . . or even sixteen.

What We Find Changes
What We Want

Has this ever happened to you? You pull up Google or Yahoo to search and type in a specific term with the best intentions of hopping on the information superhighway, pulling over at the first stop that has the materials you need, gassing up with those factoids, and heading home. Then a funny thing happens: you skim through the choices that come up for the term and find a tangential link—not quite the information you were looking for—that is too intriguing to ignore. You click on the not-quite-what-you-wanted link, which leads to more not-really-relevant links and still more tangents. Many clicks and minutes later, you find yourself on some virtual dirt road, far, far away from your original term and goals for the search. These detours only seem to reinforce random searching, because the tangents may be more interesting than the original query.

It happens to me all the time, and it turns out we're not alone in our search process. There is a whole body of research by Marcia Bates and others that documents how and why we are attracted away from our original questions when we search the Net. The theory is that "what we find changes what we want."

We know fostering independence in literacy workshops isn't about getting students to sit quietly at desks, dutifully filling out worksheets. Heck, in this day and age there are probably ways to train chimps to do that. So what is independence about? Perhaps the greatest challenge these days is arranging lessons, materials, and options in classrooms so that what students find as they read and write on their own changes what they want—and so allows them to move independently, one step at a time, down a path where they are lifelong literacy learners, constantly challenging themselves to try new genres, authors, and ideas.

Reference

Bates, Marcia. September 12, 2002. "Towards an Integrated Model of Information Seeking and Search." Keynote, The Fourth International Conference on Information Needs. Lisbon, Portugal.

Please Don't Pardon the Interruption

It's one of the few lessons from my senior high school English class that remains fresh in my memory to this day. Mr. Wylde brought in dozens of artwork prints by Vincent van Gogh. As we pored over the images, he read bits of Van Gogh's biography. Even the most jaded high schooler couldn't help but be fascinated by the details of someone so creatively unique he would saw off his own ear. We talked about the vivid landscapes, still lifes, and Van Gogh's mental illness. The high point came about ten minutes before the end of the period, when Mr. Wylde played Don McLean's haunting ballad "Vincent" (also known as "Starry Starry Night"), to show us how words could paint images every bit as vibrant as the artwork in our hands.

And then, midway through the song the intercom buzzed, and the school secretary droned on with an announcement about a bus schedule change. Some of us physically jumped, so abrupt was the return to the reality of sitting in the classroom, controlled by and waiting for the next bell. The mood and teaching point were lost as the song played on. Mr. Wylde looked like he wanted to cut off his own ear for just a moment, but then he shrugged and told us the night's homework.

Visiting classrooms each year, I've always been struck by the different standards for interruptions. Some schools have virtually no bells or intercom use, and they still run smoothly. Others have a continuous, insistent background of beeps and disembodied voices. True story: A middle school teacher in a nearby town spent years complaining about constant intercom interruptions. Finally, the last spring of his career, he undertook a research project for two weeks. Every time the intercom beeped with an announcement, he stopped what he was doing, wrote the time and content of the announcement on a Post-it, and set it aside. After ten days, he invited the principal and assistant principal to view more than 250 Post-its lined up neatly in rows across an entire wall of his classroom. On one day alone, there had been nearly 50 unscheduled announcements. His legacy to the school was a change in the announcements policy. The new procedures the administration implemented within a month cut interruptions by more than 80 percent.

When is the last time your school revisited its policy for intercom use and interruptions? Teachers spend a lot of time early in the school year getting consistent literacy routines in place, yet much of this work is undermined by these distractions. It can be hard to break a trigger-happy central office of the impulse to hit the intercom button, but nothing might have a greater effect this fall in creating a sense of calm, focus, and purpose in reading and writing workshops at your school.

Things Change

"To tell you the truth, it wasn't the greatest."

I was chatting with my friend Sean, comparing notes on our experiences in graduate school. He has a doctorate in physics, and we were discussing a seminar he had during his last year of coursework. He was explaining how through a quirk in scheduling and enrollments, he was the only student in a required class. There was no possibility it wouldn't be offered, and the professor was one of the best-known researchers in the field. I was marveling at his luck, but Sean explained it wasn't as ideal as it sounded. "The classroom was a small lecture hall, so I still had to sit on a riser. He still gave his regular presentation each week using the projector and chalkboard." I was amazed. "You were the only student, and he still had you sitting in a lecture hall? Same notes, same presentation he used when he taught the course for dozens?"

"Yep. I even had to raise my hand whenever I had a question." I still chuckle at that image in my head of the lone student in a lecture hall raising his hand to get the attention of his professor. What could be more ideal for a teacher than the chance to sit at a table or in a comfortable office, sharing your knowledge with only one student? Isn't that the teaching situation we all dream of?

Sean's story is a funny and sad reminder to me of how we get locked into routines, so much so that we have trouble adjusting to new circumstances even when our situation has changed dramatically for the better. We all live the reality of making adjustments when situations deteriorate—when there are budget cuts, we're forced to adjust, reallocate, and make do. For just a moment, think about the opposite reality. Sometimes our situation actually improves—slowly, incrementally, so much so that we're hardly even aware that these big, good changes mean we're ready for some drastic adjustments to our routines.

For example, my friend Jennifer Allen was planning a daylong inservice event for her teachers last fall. These programs are built upon the premise that teachers need to learn new things from new people, or someone designated as an "expert" from outside the school community. It's one of Jen's jobs as a literacy specialist to take a lead role in putting these programs together. When she began to take the pulse of the district to figure out needs, Jen quickly realized that the best practices she had been advocating for years had become the norm in most classrooms. If anything, there were so many fine creative variations of these practices in place that it was impossible for teachers to find the time to share all the excellent activities in their classrooms with their colleagues.

Once Jen realized how much instruction had changed over the past few years in the district, she knew it was time for a new inservice routine. She enlisted teachers to present mini-workshops on innovations of their choice from their classrooms, and came up with a schedule for quick rotations so participants could try out and experience as many of these mini-workshops as possible. The result? Teachers said it was the best inservice offered by the district in years—they had never learned or enjoyed their colleagues more than they did that day.

Although it's encouraging and essential to take a moment and celebrate success, it's probably more important to take more than a moment to ponder how those successes need to change your classroom and school routines. Are students more independent during workshops? Maybe it's time to eliminate a few of those check-in routines or process minilessons you've used since the start of the year. Is there a routine or lesson you could put in their place that fosters even more independence, or a greater sense of community? That lonely professor with his lone student missed an opportunity of a lifetime for a connection with a student. Don't get so locked into routines you've had for years that you miss yours.

Bumps in the Road

The art of progress is to preserve order amid change and to preserve change amid order.

Alfred North Whitehead

A few months ago I wrote about my daughter, Dee, taking a driver's education course and receiving her learner's permit. Dee insisted on taking the course right after her 15th birthday, as soon as she was eligible. A full year before she could take the test for her driver's license, she was eager to hit the road. She loved the class, and took the wheel every time we got in the car in the weeks after she received her learner's permit.

But a funny thing happened a couple of months after Dee began driving. She spent a few weeks out of state this summer, unable to drive during that time. Before she left, there were a couple of disagreements about what music she could listen to while driving (and how loud it could be). The transition from taking the advice of a certified instructor to listening to her parents for guidance wasn't completely smooth. By midsummer, my husband and I were the ones nagging Dee to take the keys and drive, quite a switch from the days right after her training.

I've talked with other parents who have children the same age, and they experience similar issues. What we're up against is the "implementation dip." When people try new things, there is often a time after the first rush and pleasure of making a change when skills level off, or even atrophy. It's hard to resist the pull to go back to what is comfortable and routine. For a veteran teacher, it may be a return to the way you've done reading groups for 20 years. For a teen driver, it may be a move back to the passenger seat, where you can plug into your iPod and listen to your tunes at any volume you please.

Michael Fullan has written extensively about the implementation dip—the drop in "performance and confidence as one encounters an innovation that requires new skills and new understandings"(National Staff Development Council *Tools*, November 2006). Simply put, things often get worse before they get better when changes are made in learning communities. These bumps in the road are a natural, expected part of any change process. October is a time in schools when new ideas, a new curriculum, or new protocols for staff meetings will be put to the test by the implementation dip. In August or September, colleagues and students will be willing to give most new routines a chance. It's only after a few weeks or months that confidence and performance may take a hit.

One of the best ways to deal with the implementation dip is to recognize and expect it. Literacy leaders can reassure colleagues and students that it's a good sign of change and growth to reach the point where you're uncomfortable or unsure about your skills, or questioning what progress is being made. Just knowing that things will improve once you get beyond the dip and the innovation becomes habit is all that is needed to push through for a few more weeks.

Are you seeing any implementation dips yet? Have you prepared your classroom or school for them? With Dee, it was a matter of firmly letting her know that she didn't have the option of not practicing her driving every week, and it's a routine now for her to drive certain routes regularly to build her practice time. In schools, literacy leaders can talk through dips and brainstorm ways to assist colleagues as they struggle with what's new. We think through and prepare for the initial resistance that is expected when making changes. But in terms of enduring improvements, it's the quiet dips in the midst that probably deserve more of our attention.

Reference
Fullan, Michael. 2007. *The New Meaning of Educational Change.* New York: Teachers College Press.

Pace, Space, and Voice

This week I visited a marvelous second-grade classroom in Portland, Oregon. As the teacher told the students it was time to move from their desks to the rug area for read aloud, she said, "Remember to monitor your pace, space, and voice." In less than 30 seconds, all 32 of these seven- and eight-year-olds had moved quietly, quickly, and efficiently to find spots on the carpet.

Pace, space, and voice. I realized in an instant that these three little words work for monitoring transitions at any age. For the youngsters, it meant not running (or dawdling), finding a place that wasn't scrunched next to a classmate (or hogging a lot of meeting-area real estate), and not being too loud in the process (yet making their voices heard if needed).

For teachers who are part of a school community, *pace* means being provided with professional development that doesn't move too fast (but also has a facilitator willing to deal with laggards). *Space* means being given room to try new things based on your own interests, or at least the opportunity to find your own way into initiatives that are required of everyone. *Voice* is perhaps the trickiest concept of all. What do you do in your school about the voices that are always the loudest? Are you harnessing technology outside meetings through logs, emails, or anonymous surveys to ensure that those who won't speak up in a group still have a chance to be heard?

Pace, space, and voice. Whatever transitions you are in the midst of in your classroom and school, I hope these three words give you a new way to help everyone monitor their progress and place in the community.

Faith, Doubt, and Effort

In *Leading from Within*, Orli Cotel from the Sierra Club writes the following:

> *I have a note stuck to my computer listing the three qualities that a Zen master once taught are necessary for great progress: great faith, great doubt, and great effort. I try to remember that when I am feeling discouraged. Doubt is a natural part of my work, sometimes even a helpful one, because it forces me to re-evaluate my positions.*
>
> (34)

What are you doubting in your work? What can you learn from those doubts? When I think of the one project where I haven't made much progress this fall, I realize I have been going it alone. I immediately think of two or three people who are experts and would be happy to help—but I haven't asked them for help. I also haven't made enough of an effort to get that project to the top of my to-do list.

Most of us in literacy education are optimists (sometimes almost to a freakish degree—we need lots of hope and a sense of humor to get through what's thrown at us daily). When doubt creeps in about progress on a particular project, it's time to rethink how I'm spending my time, and with whom I'm spending it. I often find that just another set of eyes and ears will give me that new perspective I need to move forward. Who is that set of eyes and ears for you?

Reference

Intrator, Sam, and Megan Scribner. 2007. *Leading from Within: Poetry that Sustains the Courage to Teach.* San Francisco: Jossey-Bass.

Playtime

This week my five-year-old nephew Max was demonstrating his latest karate moves to me—double roundhouse kicks. I complimented him, and then mentioned that it was great that he had his older brother, Michael, to play karate with anytime he wanted. Max looked a bit insulted, and replied, "Aunt Brenda, we don't PLAY karate. We DO karate."

Max knows the difference between playing and doing. Though he loves karate more than anything, he knows the "doing" of karate has involved more than two years of lessons. It's much more formal and systematic than the 30-foot-long blue worm they were constructing in the basement from plastic for fun, or the club they were setting up for their new tree house this week.

As I thought about what Max said, I realized how little time there is for adults in schools to play with new ideas and possibilities for their classrooms. Almost everything is "doing"—putting in place new systems and programs, with targets and measures.

Have you made any time this year for professional play? To finally bring in that digital camera and play with snapping shots of students or colleagues at work, with no agenda for what you'll do with the photos other than enjoy them? Is there something you've always wanted to try, whether it's Poetry Friday or a regular nature walk with kids, that is open-ended enough to qualify as play? As artist Lucia Capocchione writes, "Play keeps us vital and alive. It gives us an enthusiasm for life that is irreplaceable. Without it, life just doesn't taste good." Amidst all the professional doing we're all so good at, I hope you make time for a little professional play—learning something or trying something with no goal or agenda other than having fun in the process.

What's Your *Wallah*?

In India it's hard to go far without coming across a *chai wallah*—a person who makes and sells fresh chai tea. It's what they do exclusively, and you can find a chai wallah on scores of street corners, by shrines, even on trains as you travel. They don't sell magazines or give shoeshines or offer any other services. They just make tea.

I realized last night I am a shortbread wallah; I made up a big batch when I was called at the last minute to bring something to an event tomorrow. I know how to make other cookies, but shortbread is what my friends ask for because I've made it so often. We all have at least one simple task or skill we have perfected over time.

I know two literacy coaches who work together in a district. One is gifted when it comes to organizing and making sense of assessment data. The other is amazingly talented at working one-on-one in classrooms with teachers, nudging them out of their comfort zones. These two coaches decided long ago to rethink their workloads, giving far more of the assessment load to the data wallah and more classroom coaching time to the conferring wallah. They are both happier in their work—wonderful collaborators with each other and their colleagues. Their bosses are delighted that they have beautifully organized data and terrific support for teachers in classrooms. The data wallah does spend some time in classrooms, and the conferring wallah has to pore over numbers now and again. But they've given themselves permission, and so has their administration, to maximize their time and minimize their burnout by doing more of what they do best.

Teachers and literacy coaches are expected to do many things well—*often far too many things well*. We excel at some tasks and muddle through many others. There is much to be gained by getting creative in reallocating responsibilities. My good friends Joan Moser and Gail Boushey ("The Sisters") work so well together in part because they respect each other's strengths. Joan has a special talent for dealing with difficult people; there's no one I'd want with me more than Gail when my computer and sound system blows up in the middle of a presentation. They have a tacit agreement that Joan is their conflict wallah and Gail is their tech wallah. Can Joan work through a software problem? Of course; I've seen her do it more than once. And I've also been there when Gail carefully and skillfully talked through an issue with someone ready to pitch a fit. Yet whenever they are together and have a choice, they immediately choose Gail to resolve tech issues and Joan to smooth over people problems.

What's your wallah? What's the wallah of the teacher next door, or the other literacy coach in your school? Can you partner and rejigger your responsibilities so that you're doing more of what you love, or at least what you do well and efficiently? One thing about those chai wallahs in India: no brew tastes exactly the same. Even when you do something well, you have your own particular flair with the task. When we watch anyone who has truly mastered a skill, we learn more than we do stumbling our way through it, alone and discouraged. Sweet tea indeed.

A Verb and a Decision

Monday morning I sat on an airplane, preparing to fly home for the Thanksgiving holiday. The pilot stood in the center aisle, giving the usual spiel about flight time and the weather back home, and rattling off the names of the co-pilot and three flight attendants.

He concluded with these words: "If there is anything we can do to make your flight more enjoyable, please let us know. We really love this airline, and we hope you'll come to love it too."

We really love what we do, and we hope you'll come to love it too.

As much as I've enjoyed my work at different schools over the years, I don't think I've ever declared myself so publicly to a large group of strangers. Love not as a feeling, but as a verb and a decision. I wondered how the mood might shift at a welcome night early in the fall for families new to the school if they heard the principal say, "Our staff really loves this school, and we hope you'll come to love it too." Or if at a literacy open house they heard you say, "I really love reading aloud to your child, and I hope you'll love it too." Or at the first mentor meeting of the year: "I love this program—it made all the difference to me when I was a new teacher, and I hope it does for you too." Or to a child, "I loved this book when I was your age—I hope you'll love it too."

Times are hard, and many in our communities are struggling. In the midst of all that, maybe we need a little less "Fasten your seat belts—it's going to be a bumpy ride" and a little more "Fasten your seat belts, and prepare to be delighted."

Winter

There's no way around it: winter is a hard season in many schools. It's a slog to get through the cold dark months with tests too long, tempers too short, and that anxiety that descends when we start wondering if we're up to this impossible task of moving this year's crop of learners forward. Not to mention the reliable arrival of the flu season and the race to get those wastebaskets nearest the kid looking the greenest.

But the winter months are also quiet ones, and they are peppered with those moments of joy when a class finally starts coming together as a community, or when a study group or grade-level team meeting has its first true belly laugh together (the gallows humor of February has some rewards). We manage to get through the winter, and we usually emerge stronger, if a bit tired.

Kinder, Gentler Literacy Leaders

It is better to be kind than to be right.

These words were spoken by my sister Mary over the holidays, in the midst of one of our family's cutthroat card games. As a matter of fact, "Cutthroat" is one of our favorite versions of pinochle. We come from the Midwest tradition of long evenings at a huge scarred oak table filled with all the leaves. Scores of cousins, aunts, uncles, and friends play euchre, pinochle, and other games of chance for hours. It's mostly laughter and fun, but occasionally an argument bursts out after a particularly feisty hand, with the players disagreeing about whether someone played their cards right.

It is better to be kind than to be right.

My sister spoke those words quietly to quickly end a disagreement between a niece and nephew at the card table, and I carried them away into the new year as my resolution. It's sometimes tough when you're sure you're right—from the research, experience, or just gut instinct—to back down in kindness and let a wrong notion pass when uttered by a colleague. But for literacy leaders, it may be one of the most important attitudes to have—a willingness to choose kindness over correcting a peer. Sometimes it is so hard to hold your tongue and let things go, in a world where everyone thinks they are an education expert.

The truth is, we do know what we're doing, and our expertise is hard won. Yet it's a gentle touch that wins colleagues and community members over, and a heavy hand that leads to stalemates. In the end, how would you prefer to be remembered—as someone who was always right, or always kind?

Bus, Bath, and Bed

Have you ever had a situation that bothered you for weeks at school, an issue you couldn't seem to resolve, only to have the solution come to you when you least expected it? I've sometimes joked to friends that I should spend all my time driving around in my car doing errands, because that's where I seem to solve all my problems.

The late psychologist Wolfgang Kohler called this the "bus, bath, and bed" phenomenon:

> *After periods during which one has actively tried to solve a problem, but has not succeeded, the sudden right orientation of the situation, and with it the solution, tend to occur at moments of extreme mental passivity . . . A well-known physicist in Scotland once told me that this kind of thing is generally recognized by physicists in Britain. "We often talk about the Three Bs," he said. "The Bus, the Bath, and the Bed. That's where the great discoveries are made in our science."*
>
> *(152)*

Anyone can harness the power of the "Three B's" for problem solving in a few practical ways. You might keep a small notepad and pen at bedside or on your car's armrest console for when those solutions emerge suddenly in traffic or almost out of a dream. (No one has invented a waterproof Post-it yet, so I'm still looking for a bath equivalent.) And in schools, the lesson for literacy leaders is often patience. Our norm is to present a problem at a meeting, with a goal of brainstorming a solution together by the end of the hour. If you can resist that urge, and present the issue with a goal of discussing possible solutions at a meeting the next day or week, your colleagues will have their own flashes of insight while sitting in traffic or dashing through their rote morning routines.

Plant a seed and give your colleagues time to mull it over. You're almost assured of getting more interesting and inspired suggestions by way of the bed, bath, or bus.

Reference
Kohler, Wolfgang. 1991. In *Free Play Improvisation in Life and Art* by Stephen Nachmanovitch. New York: Tarcher Books.

Clearing the Way

On Wednesday afternoon we had a blizzard here in rural Maine. Since the storm wasn't scheduled to start till after noon, school wasn't canceled. (If we canceled school every time snow was forecast, most New England kids would end up homeschooled.)

The forecast was accurate, and by one o'clock the snow was heavy, falling at a rate of an inch or two an hour. I drove a couple of miles to the nearest school bus stop to transport my child and others home, barely making it up a slick hill. I wondered how in the world all the local districts would manage to get thousands of children home that day.

And then I spied a bright yellow vehicle—not the bus, but a large plow and sand machine, making its way down the road, clearing a path for the bus. Three minutes later, the bus arrived. I'm sure the scene was repeated at bus stops in communities throughout the region, because in the face of a pretty awful blizzard, every child made it home safely that day.

As I watched the snowplow pass, I thought about how we can't control the weather, but we can control our response to it. When I think of the colleagues I've valued the most through the years, many times the relationship was cemented when they or I dropped our plans, rolled up our sleeves, and helped each other through one professional storm or another. The challenge is knowing when it's a true crisis that requires setting aside plans for a colleague. There is always someone on staff who is perpetually frazzled, waiting till beyond the last minute to accomplish anything. They have muddled through life assuming someone will always be there to rescue them. We break our routines for them at our peril.

But I also suspect there is a new teacher you work with who at this very moment is struggling quietly, with no idea how to deal with a difficult parent or the mountain of assessment data before her. Do you have any time this week to clear a path for her? It's those make-or-break moments that often mark whether or not young teachers stay in the profession.

First-Class Touches

What kind of environment do you learn best in? Over the past few months I've been working with hotels and resorts all over the country, reserving space for the Choice Literacy summer leadership workshops and institutes.

It's a funny thing: when I mentioned to event coordinators that the workshops are for teachers, not one said, "Oh, wait—teachers?! We've got a dreary, moldy space in the basement reserved just for people like you." Everyone knew our group would expect the best facilities they had to offer, and that's what we got.

I think we've come to expect much less than we should when it comes to the "basics" of what anyone needs to learn—adults as well as children. Shelley Harwayne writes about this in *Going Public*:

> *The teaching profession has never been honored with any first-class touches. But a quiet room used for staff development can become truly elegant when it contains a tray of cookies, a basket of fresh fruit, a pot of good coffee with real milk. It can be made elegant with the addition of carefully duplicated articles, well-thought-out calendars, and invitations to attend relevant conferences.*

(254)

First-class touches in school-based literacy professional development programs needn't be expensive, but they do demonstrate a sense of care and handcrafting of the learning experience for teachers and children. Small items, seemingly insignificant, can make all the difference in a teacher moving from being intrigued to actually testing out a new idea in his or her classroom.

I've been inspired over the years by the first-class touches of Jennifer Allen, a literacy coach who contributes frequently to Choice Literacy. She transformed an ugly basement room (which was dank and dreary) at her school into a charming "literacy room" chock-full of resources and inviting spaces for teachers. Her advice for literacy leaders looking to add some first-class touches to study groups on a "coach" budget:

- Save room in your budget for small items from the local dollar or office supply store like baskets for books, Post-its, inexpensive frames for children's writing or quotes, and so on, so that when these needs arise from a study group discussion, you can purchase them for colleagues.

- Materials tied directly to study group themes are a nice surprise gift at any time during the year (i.e., handheld tape recorders for a fluency group, dry-erase boards and markers for a word study group, colorful individual journals for a writer's notebook group).

- Use book club bonus points for a small fridge to house a supply of bottled water and light snacks, with a coffeemaker on top. This encourages teachers to pause, browse, and chat with colleagues as they look through resources.

- Coffee is great, but fresh water is really appreciated by teachers who are tired and thirsty at the start of late-afternoon meetings.

- Distribute purchase orders for books from the nicest local bookstore at the end of the summer or just before a school break, rather than just asking for lists of books from teachers to requisition. This gets teachers out into the bookstores browsing—a lovely environment for anyone to explore—and the experience inevitably introduces teachers to new books and new ways to display books in their classrooms.

- If you live nearby, host the education technicians (assistants) at your home for a breakfast discussion of needs and goals one morning. Platters of baked goods from a local bakery aren't expensive, and these colleagues can easily be overlooked when it comes to honoring their contribution and building community.

Reference

Harwayne, Shelley. 1999. *Going Public*. Portsmouth, NH: Heinemann.

Why We Love Lists

My parents are celebrating their 50th anniversary soon, so they decided to take all 27 of their children, grandchildren, and great-grandchildren on a cruise for the holidays. A couple of months ago, my ever-subtle mom mentioned casually on the phone, "It's your first cruise, Brenda—you'll find the booklet they send along very helpful." I had to chuckle, because I knew what she was concerned about. Up here in the willywags of Maine, clean Bean boots and jeans without holes in them qualify as "business casual" dress. Combine that with my innate lack of any fashion sense, and I think she was afraid our country bumpkin branch of the family would show up looking like lumberjacks at the captain's table. (Hey, we would have worn new plaid shirts and fleece for the occasion!)

Last month brought a couple more hints, until this week Mom finally just sent a mass email to everyone: "Don't wait till the last minute to pack—make sure to read the dress code in the guide."

Sure enough, the little booklet has a great checklist on page 6. It not only designates which dinners are "formal" or "informal" but defines exactly what types of dresses and suits fit each category. All in less than a page, with a phrase or two definition of what qualifies as appropriate.

The checklist reminded me how much I appreciate a good list, and how much of a literacy leader's job involves "breaking it down" for others. Whenever I have insomnia because I have too much to do, I get up and write out a list of the eight to ten things I need to get done over the next week on the project that's keeping me up. Then I can finally go back to sleep. I thought I was the only one with this little quirk, till I discovered a couple of teacher friends who have the same habit. We can remind people of deadlines; we can even use adjectives like *formal* for dress or *formative* for an assessment to explain what is expected. But it doesn't mean our colleagues know what we're talking about, or even where to begin chunking a big project into manageable smaller tasks. This is especially true for colleagues who are new to the school or district and have little sense of the local norms.

Of course, we've all seen those ridiculous assessments or observation checklists that are 13 pages long with 346 items on them. They are a reminder that there is an art to constructing a checklist—providing enough detail so that readers have the information they need, but not at a level that overwhelms them or insults their intelligence.

One of the best gifts you can give the colleagues you assist is advice on what needs to be done, and when, for a big deadline that looms a month or two down the road. Veteran teachers may not need the help, but novice teachers often really appreciate the concrete simplicity of a good checklist. And if you find the checklist is running onto a second page, with more than a dozen items, you probably haven't broken down the project into small enough chunks. It's a good test for any of us: if we can't break it down into a simple list, how can we expect others new to the task to do it themselves?

Coffee Guerillas

Last week I was on the road with a video crew, spending lots of time stuck in airports waiting for the weather to clear. During one delay I stopped at the newsstand to get something to read, and noticed a paper Starbucks coffee cup left on top of a vending machine.

As I reached to swipe the cup and throw it in the trash, I realized it hadn't been left by a litterbug. Someone had placed the cup carefully so that anyone purchasing a newspaper couldn't help but notice the quote printed on the back of it, from the 1998 Teacher of the Year:

> *A child's mind isn't a blank slate; it's more of a jungle. Each time a parent helps a toddler read, the child is walked through this jungle from one side to the other. Trip after trip, a seemingly impossible passage becomes a well-worn path. Children sent to kindergarten skipping merrily along this path to literacy fare far better than those sent to school with machetes.*
>
> *Keith Mastrion, "Reading Man" and*
> *1998 National Teacher of the Year*

Let the politicians have their splashy reading reform initiatives or the new superintendents their flashy PowerPoint presentations on how they will move schools further and faster than ever before. Real change happens one teacher, one student, one coffee cup at a time. We see words that matter, and we find a way to pass them on. And slowly, what we all believe about kids, literacy, and learning changes. Literacy activism and good coffee: now, there's a combination worth savoring.

The Elevator Pitch

What is your job? Why is it important?

Have you ever had to answer these questions on the spot? We're in the midst of budget season in schools, when administrators crunch numbers and everyone makes funding requests that will start cycling their way through committees and school boards. If your position or a favorite literacy project may end up in the red zone for possible elimination, it might be time to craft an "elevator pitch."

The term *elevator pitch* comes from the business world, and the premise is simple: if a stranger in an elevator asked you to describe your job or project, what would you say? What are the most succinct, concise, and intriguing few sentences you can string together that explain the work thoroughly, but still can be conveyed in the time it takes an elevator to move up or down a few floors?

The beauty of a well-crafted elevator pitch is that once you have it, it's not hard to remember because it's so short. When you find yourself chatting in line at the grocery store with a parent, or on the soccer field sidelines with a school board member, you can run through it naturally when the topic of your favorite literacy initiative or your daily responsibilities comes up.

These short pitches are especially important if you have one of the literacy leadership positions that have cropped up recently with titles no one outside of schools (or sometimes inside) can understand. How many people outside of education really understand what a "literacy coach" does? What's a "teacher on special assignment" or "curriculum support teacher"? How do you explain the role of an "assistant superintendent for literacy professional development"?

There are literally hundreds of different job descriptions among the subscribers to this newsletter for literacy leaders, and I suspect the more unusual or new the title is, the more likely the job will be targeted for cuts during lean budget times. And if you want to move from a simple job title, like "fourth-grade teacher," to something more complicated, like "team leader for literacy development," an elevator pitch can help you create a winning argument for taking on more of a leadership role in your school.

Elevator pitches are simple, but they sure aren't easy to construct. I've been writing my elevator pitch about what I do at Choice Literacy for more than a year, and it's just about perfect . . . as long as the elevator is traveling at least 57 floors!

To Build a Fire

How cold is it in your neck of the woods? Much of North America is in the midst of a bitterly frigid stretch of weather. I awoke this morning to a reading of 27 degrees below zero (at least according to the ancient thermometer on our deck). With the windchill, temperatures feel like -45°F. My husband and I compared notes, and we're fairly certain this is the coldest weather we've experienced in the 20 years we've lived in rural Maine.

Whenever there is a cold snap and I find myself hunkered down or trudging through the snow, I think about one of my favorite short stories, Jack London's *To Build a Fire*. I haven't read it in many years, but the images from it stick with me, especially the ones in this passage:

> *Fifty degrees below zero stood for a bite of frost that hurt and that must be guarded against by the use of mittens, ear flaps, warm moccasins, and thick socks. Fifty degrees below zero was to him just precisely fifty degrees below zero. That there should be anything more to it than that was a thought that never entered his head.*

As he turned to go on, he spat speculatively. There was a sharp, explosive crackle that startled him. He spat again. And again, in the air, before it could fall to the snow, the spittle crackled. He knew that at fifty below spittle crackled on the snow, but this spittle had crackled in the air. Undoubtedly it was colder than fifty below—how much colder he did not know.

(105)

It's that crack in the air, like a gunshot, that wakes the man up and makes him realize he'll have to give more thought to the cold throughout the day. Everything has changed because of how low the temperature has dipped, and his survival depends upon dealing well with the changes in the landscape.

This week I sat in on an assessment study group in Waterville, Maine. I couldn't help but think of how things have changed when it comes to assessment and testing in schools as I listened to these teachers struggle to make connections between their teaching and the state exams.

Much as we keep trying to make the relentless testing fit into our classroom landscapes of workshops, inquiry, high-quality literature, and authentic learning, there's not really much of a match. Whatever we do to prepare students for timed exams—from treating tests as another "genre," to holding schoolwide pep rallies to up everyone's enthusiasm for No. 2 pencils and bubble sheets—there is no getting around the nagging sense that too much of testing these days is about survival. And as long as testing is about fighting for the survival of anything—of our schools on "failing lists," or our kids who are struggling with performance anxiety, or even our own self-esteem as educators—it will never really be about learning.

So we gear up and make do, turning to each other for tips, strategies, and the good humor we need to get through the slog of the testing season. I know before long that ancient thermometer on my deck will be framed by a basket of flowers and registering warmth again. There will be real learning and energizing curriculum again in the weeks beyond the tests too. We know this, and it keeps us moving forward with optimism.

Reference

London, Jack. 2008. *To Build a Fire and Other Stories.* New York: Digireads.com.

The Truth About Community

Are you a fan of the acknowledgments in books? I love what acknowledgments reveal about any author before I even get into the meat of their writing.

Do they acknowledge their spouse? Their dog? Are they emotional? Clinical? As I read the laundry list of thanks, I see the author's personal and professional community (and I have to admit my evil twin Not-Nice Brenda is intrigued by who should be on the list . . . but is mysteriously absent).

My all-time favorite acknowledgment may be the co-authors who thanked their therapist for getting them through the many times they were fighting while drafting their manuscript, or not speaking to each other at all. The topic of their book? How to build effective, nurturing communities. You might think their honesty about fierce arguments during the process would make me question their advice on community building. Instead, it made me respect them more.

Community building is the hardest work we do. It's often been said that you know you're really a part of a community only when there's at least one person in it you just can't stand. Only then do you know whether you've found enough common ground. The path to that place will always be marked by differences in beliefs, styles, and attitudes.

What we're after is true commitment and collaboration, which is probably why you became a literacy leader in the first place. Beneath all the language and history that divides us in any school community, there is a profound, shared vision that we can and must make a difference in students' lives. We wouldn't be here if we didn't believe that, and we're willing to accept the challenge of a few dust-ups (or sessions with therapists) along the way to get there together.

Gorillas in Our Midst

Researchers Daniel Simons and Christopher Chabris did a famous experiment some years ago. They asked their research subjects to perform a simple task: watch a video of a group of students passing basketballs, and keep a silent tally of how many passes were made.

Moments after the start of the video, someone dressed in a gorilla suit walks slowly into the cluster of students tossing the basketballs, stopping in the middle of the action to beat its chest and demand attention. The students keep throwing the basketballs back and forth, and the gorilla eventually ambles out of the scene.

Amazingly, 50 percent of the research study participants did not recall the presence of the gorilla when asked about it after the video ended. The experiment demonstrates how when we focus on a task, we often completely miss striking objects and events around us.

I've been thinking about these "gorillas in our midst" as I've been following Andrea Smith's advice for slowing down and actually enjoying the small break of a fire drill. Andrea explained the routine she's developed for fire drills that helps her enjoy her students and teaching more. It's four short words designed to help anyone pause and see more in the world around them:

Breathe. Smile. Notice. Enjoy.

We don't have fire drills here at Choice Literacy (that, and not being forced to eat lunch at 10:30 AM, are probably the biggest perks of not working full time in a public school). So, I've been trying to take Andrea's advice once a day, just to see what happens. It's truly amazing how those few seconds wake you up and help you notice remarkable things right in front of your nose. And it's hard not to enjoy the new view when you've plastered a silly grin on your face the moment before you look. I even tried it in the doctor's office yesterday, and noticed for the first time a display of children's artwork in a corner of the waiting room.

By the way, children are naturals at the *breathe smile notice enjoy* habit. It's why transitions can be so difficult for adults in classrooms, and so blissful for many kids. They love the opportunity a transition gives for noticing, smiling, and mixing things up a little with their classmates. It's ironic that we have to squelch those tendencies for students to get off routine during transitions so that we don't end up with chaos, even as we have to push ourselves to stay more open to the moment.

Reference

Simons, Daniel, and Christopher Chabris. 1995. "Gorillas in Our Midst: Sustained Inattentional Blindness for Dynamic Events." *British Journal of Developmental Psychology*: 28(9) 113–142.

"Good" Teachers

Some years back I was leading a professional development initiative at a local school, involving novice teachers and their mentors. I was at the school almost every day, forming cordial relationships, visiting classrooms, and coordinating study groups.

I thought everything was going well, and then I was brought up short by a quote I read in the book *Mentor/Teacher*. The essay was written as a plea from teachers to the supervisors who lead them, and this is the quote that stopped me in my tracks:

> *I have a right to be who I am, as a person and as a teacher. My experiences, history, career stage, and current life demands make me who I am. And although I don't always say or believe this, I like who I am. I am unique and proud of my work, but I am fragile. I work in a world where everything is changing, constantly, daily, faster every year. I want to grow and be a better teacher, to be allowed to make the mistakes that come with real change. That alone qualifies me to be a strong mentor of beginning teachers.*

Any talk of "the best teachers" or "bad teachers" hurts deeply. On any one day, I'm both; I'll never be as good as Beth or Roger down the hall, but I'm trying. I need to know that you will not talk negatively about me or my methods once you get back in the car, or are at another school. Do not ask me to become destabilized in front of my students, my teacher candidate, or my peers; don't push me further than I'm ready to go. As I learn, I need to maintain face, if not always control.

(141)

I could feel my face getting red as I reread these words silently and they began to sink in. I knew the anonymous teacher writing those words; I was that anonymous teacher earlier in my career. Though I rarely spoke of "bad" teachers, making proclamations about what "good" or "the best" teachers do was something that happened a dozen times a day in my work.

I read this quote aloud at the next mentor meeting, and talked about how I needed to change my language. The air in the room shifted after those words. Before, the staff had been polite, quiet, clearly tired after a long day. But after discussing the quote, I could feel a new buzz, a whiff of possibility that we were trying for a different kind of collaboration among mentors and colleagues.

The feeling of being judged as a teacher is continual, and it probably goes all the way back to teacher preparation programs, when so many absolutes are presented as "good" or "bad" practice. It isn't easy to change the words we use routinely, because they reflect thinking patterns that are ingrained.

If you're a literacy leader in any capacity—a mentor, coach, study group coordinator, principal—you have to measure your words. If we don't measure our words, the risk is that the teachers we work with will measure themselves by them, in ways that inhibit or hurt our ability to change and grow together as learners.

Reference
Graham, Peg, et al. 1999. *Mentor/Teacher*. New York: Teachers College Press.

The Right Tool at the Right Time

This past week 30 new inches of snow fell in our area of rural Maine. I know—I've written about the snow before, and if you're sick of reading about it, just think of how tired I am of living in it. I figure writing about the weather at least puts my readers in Australia and Florida in a good mood as they don their shorts and head out for the day.

Anyway, after we had the driveway cleared, my first stop was at one of those big-box hardware chain stores to pick up a roof rake. For those of you who have the good fortune of never needing this tool, it's exactly as it sounds: a rake on a long, lightweight pole that allows you to scrape the snow and ice off your roof before it all comes sliding down on your head.

I knew I would never be able to find the rake on my own in the huge store, so I walked straight to the clerk at the information booth. She shook her head sadly when I questioned her. "We've been out of roof rakes for almost a month. You can't imagine how many people have come through that door asking for them." I figured this might be good luck on my part, because surely this meant more would be coming in soon. "Oh no—we've moved on to spring merchandise," she replied. "Just look at the displays; we won't have much available for snow removal again for nine months." I glanced around and saw that I was surrounded by patio furniture, deck umbrellas, and lawn mowers. Just beyond the clerk's booth was a large array of small flowers in pots waiting to be planted in gardens, already wilting under the fluorescent lights.

The clerk and I looked at each other and burst out laughing. Neither of us will be relaxing on a chaise lounge in the garden with a gin and tonic, watching our tulips bloom, anytime soon. We have more than five feet of snow on the ground, and even if it miraculously melts next week, the earth is frozen solid. Spring is just around the corner somewhere—just not in this particular corner of rural Maine.

Some central office geniuses for that hardware chain at a location thousands of miles away are dictating what must be displayed and stocked, even though they are far removed from their workers who actually live near the stores. I'm not knocking the value of the business. Since it opened last year, we've purchased all sorts of materials from them and even had their crew remodel our kitchen. But isn't the primary job of a hardware store to supply the right tool at the right time?

Literacy leaders always feel that tension of being tugged toward the goals, mandates, and calendars designed by others who are sometimes far removed from life on the ground in classrooms. If you're feeling pulled in too many directions, it never hurts to ask yourself, What's the most important thing I need to do, every day, without fail?

There are probably a thousand different right answers to that question. One of them is certainly putting the right book at the right time into the right hands. When the school gets engulfed in test prep craziness and a colleague or student melts down, *Testing Miss Malarkey* by Judy Finchler might be a perfect fit. When a coworker takes a big risk in changing her curriculum and you're the first to know, *Walk On!* by Marla Frazee is a funny and uplifting pep talk in the guise of a children's book about first steps. We are always reading with others in mind, stocking our mental shelves with the tools people in our community will need to get through any rough patch.

I hope you're treating yourself to lots of book browsing time these days, no matter how many other demands there are for your attention. Sometimes burying ourselves in books feels like a guilty pleasure, since we're paid to do what we love best. But it's not just reading—it's taking inventory, meeting needs, and always connecting others to worlds beyond those in front of our noses.

References
Finchler, Judy. 2003. *Testing Miss Malarkey.* New York: Walker Books for Young Readers.
Frazee, Marla. 2006. *Walk On!* New York: Harcourt Children's Books.

Feature Bloat

Yesterday my friend Jen and I were chatting when we discovered coincidentally that we'd upgraded to the same new cell phone over the holidays. Jen loves the phone; I don't. I won't give you the brand name, but here's a hint: if you want to build up the muscles in your thumbs, this is the phone for you!

To understand our reactions, you need a little context. Jen received her phone as a gift, and it was a present she really wanted. What she prizes about the phone is the feature that allows her to check and delete emails on quick breaks throughout the day. "It makes me feel so much less overwhelmed when I open my email at the end of the day and there is so little there," she told me.

On the other hand, I had to get a new phone because my ancient cell phone looked like it had been thrown into a grinder and then left out in the rain after years of abuse. The thing was nearly obsolete, but then again, I'm the kind of person who would be happily pecking away on my Apple IIe if the world hadn't made me upgrade my computer a dozen times since 1982. I like the ease and convenience that technology can bring, but I also always feel like I'm stumbling my way through life trying to understand the latest new gadgets.

Jen and I both agreed that a problem with the new phone is "feature bloat": there are 34 icons on the tiny screen. The first one is for a social network neither Jen nor I (nor most business professionals over 40 who are the prime audience for the phone) ever use. The fourth icon is for messages, and somewhere beyond that is the link to stored phone numbers. Messages and phone numbers—those two features are the ones I use 99 percent of the time, and it's irritating to have to squint at 32 icons I don't need to find them.

As Jen and I were chatting, I thought about how easy it is to fall prey to feature bloat when you're designing professional development offerings across the year in a school or district. In our quest to provide a range of options, tailored to different needs, schedules, and interests, we may be fostering some "opportunity bloat" among our colleagues.

When we offer a new study group or workshop, there will be people on staff who are sincerely grateful because it's exactly the option they need at that moment in their lives and teaching. But some of the Apple IIe lovers among us will see it only as yet another of the 48 (or 148!) opportunities they barely have time to notice on the calendar, let alone participate in this year. These are the folks who pine for the days when you could show up for the monthly staff meeting, knitting in hand, and know you'd fulfilled your PD duty.

119

How can you avoid feature bloat when it comes to the professional development offerings you're providing? You may know the community literacy breakfast next month is the most important literacy event of the year, if only because half the school board, the mayor, and many parents who never come to anything else will be there. But does everyone else know why it matters more than the study group, book room reorganization meeting, or team meeting on the calendar for the same day or week?

It's never easy to streamline and prioritize offerings when audiences and needs vary so much among educators, but you might begin by asking yourself these questions:

> How have I helped colleagues decide which offerings are most important for them? How do I help them balance these priorities with those of the whole school or district?

> What is our process for pruning professional development opportunities that no longer meet our needs?

> How flexible am I in allowing and providing alternatives to attendance at events?

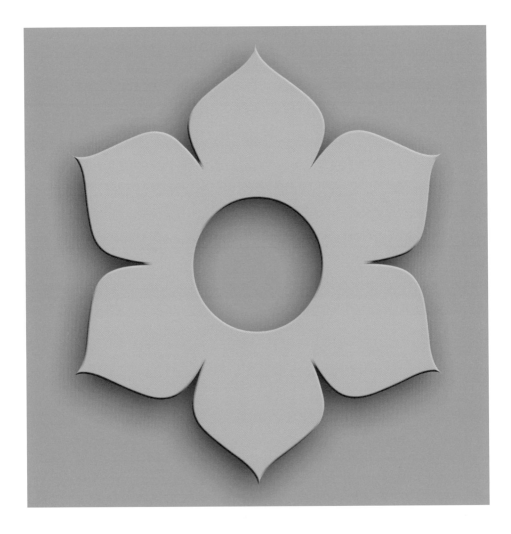

Spring

Here in Maine, it seems like it takes forever for spring to arrive. I look longingly at the flowers sprouting outside the studios of morning news shows in New York. We don't experience spring until late April or May. And then it is time to pay attention. The branches that have been bare so long sprout tiny buds, unfurling with the lightest shade of lime green, darkening ever so slightly every day for a few weeks. Voila! It seems I blink and it's full-on summer.

We all wait and long for spring in schools, and when it finally arrives, it's a rush to fit everything in and, most important, to pay attention. There are so many moments and experiences with students we want to capture, to savor before summer resets the clock on another year. We blink, and the year is over.

Careful Gardeners

Just back from a quick trip to the Pacific Northwest, where we filmed some fabulous makeovers of classroom libraries, book rooms, and storage areas we'll be featuring in a "literacy spring cleaning" series soon. But what struck me most was what was going on outside the classrooms. Gardens are in full bloom in Seattle, and the lush flowers reminded me of how our little corner in Maine is always late to see spring each year.

How ironic that the start of the gardening and testing seasons overlap in most schools. Gardening reconnects many teachers to the natural world, and at the same time test after test in our classrooms couldn't feel more surreal.

The late educational researcher Lawrence Stenhouse noted that the difference between the teacher and the large-scale policy maker is like the difference between a farmer with a huge agricultural business to maintain and the "careful gardener" tending a backyard plot. It's a quote I've loved for a long time, especially when contrasting the goals of high test scores with my goals as a teacher:

In agriculture the equation of invested input against gross yield is all: it does not matter if individual plants fail to thrive or die so long as the cost of saving them is greater than the cost of losing them . . . This does not apply to the careful gardener whose labour is not costed, but a labour of love. He wants each of his plants to thrive, and he can treat each one individually. Indeed he can grow a hundred different plants in his garden and differentiate his treatment of each, pruning his roses, but not his sweet peas. Gardening rather than agriculture is the analogy for education.

(27)

When you care about each and every plant thriving, it changes the way you view everything. Rereading this quote reminded me of the mutual passions of teachers and gardeners. When the world pushes us to move faster and harder in schools, the careful gardener often has to do just the opposite.

Reference

Stenhouse, Lawrence. 1999. In *Living the Questions* by Ruth Shagoury Hubbard and Brenda Power. Portland, ME: Stenhouse Publishers.

Faithful to a Fault

> Working on a new idea is kind of like getting married. Then a new idea comes along and you think, "Man I'd really like to go out with her." But you can't. At least not until the old idea is finished.
>
> **Stephen King**

Coming up with new ideas to try in our classrooms or schools is almost never a problem—it's finding a way to end gracefully events or activities that no longer have the value they once did for students or colleagues. That's what's hard for many of us.

Literacy leaders walk a fine line. We've all worked with colleagues who jump willy-nilly from creating one splashy event or curriculum overhaul to the next, trying to drag us all along with them. Traditions and annual celebrations matter— they build a sense of community and closure.

Yet as you look at your spring calendar of events, ask yourself if there is an annual gathering on it that isn't as essential as it once was. Is there a literacy night for families with falling attendance? A mentor celebration during a packed week that would work better late in the summer or early in the fall? One more end-of-the-year recognition ceremony for kids that is one too many? Sometimes these events begin with grant money or to address a specific need at a moment in time. Years later they may still show up every spring on the calendar, even if they are only limping along when it comes to interest and support.

One of the biggest challenges for literacy leaders is finding a kind and fair way to turn away from ideas that have run their course, to make room for new ones. We cancel events with a long school history at our peril, and it shouldn't be done lightly. If we dismiss the hard-won curricular changes made by a colleague over years, we shouldn't expect her to put much energy or attention into our suggestions.

Stephen King's metaphor about marriage in the lead quote is humorous to those of us who live near him in Maine, because he's been happily married for more than 40 years to his college sweetheart. Fidelity is prized in all aspects of our lives for a reason. But when anyone looks at the overstuffed spring calendars of many schools, they might wonder why we choose to be faithful to so very many end-of-year traditions.

When We Were Little

Tell me a story from when you were yittle.

My daughter could never pronounce the *l* in *little* when she was a preschooler. When she was bored or we were driving around in the car, she would often pipe up with a request for a tale from when I was "yittle" like her. She loved hearing about the scheme I had with my sisters for selling tadpoles door to door to earn money one summer (that really didn't work out well), my best friends, the trouble I got into . . . and the teachers who made their mark on me.

As busy as this time is for teachers, you've probably done most everything you need to do for a successful year already with students and colleagues. Classroom communities are thriving, and there's a quiet sense of accomplishment as you close out your professional development offerings for the year.

We're greedy. It's not enough for most of us to do the job well—we want to be remembered. Decades from now, our students will have children of their own, and those children will ask for stories. We want at least a few of those to come from our classrooms.

Have you told your students and colleagues enough stories from when you were little this year? For my daughter, *little* meant her size. For our students and colleagues, it means when we were in their shoes, with less experience and fewer skills, and often more enthusiasm than common sense. The most memorable stories often begin with a failure—the bigger the better.

Nothing binds us to others more than the stories we share, especially those that make us laugh together. So before the year rushes to an end, I hope you'll find time to share at least a few more anecdotes from when you were little—just learning to read, write, teach, and lead. And when your students aren't little anymore, they may still be passing your wisdom along.

What We Save

We recently filmed a funny exchange as three teachers reorganized a storage area. Carrie, the second-year teacher who volunteered to have her room decluttered, was resisting the plea from two veteran teachers to discard a very large box that was taking up a lot of space.

The box contained borders for bulletin boards marking every possible occasion or theme: shamrocks, Santas, fireworks, turkeys, circus clowns. Carrie explained, "I thought I could use those to change out the boards and dress them up all year. Other teachers gave them to me and I picked up some from Goodwill." She then sheepishly admitted that she never had changed the borders on her bulletin boards even once all year, and finally the box was tossed . . . or passed along to an unsuspecting new teacher or back to Goodwill. (It may be our profession's version of that one lone fruitcake that is gifted and regifted all through December.)

Why oh why do we save so many things we never use? I remember reading a story about the actress Glenn Close, who had a pair of size 2 jeans from her youth she saved for almost 20 years before finally throwing them away. I imagine this rich and famous actress dragging those tiny jeans all over the world. Surely if she ever got that thin again she could afford to buy a new pair!

The excess baggage we carry sometimes represents the gap between who we are and the nagging sense of who we think we should be. If only we were the kind of teacher who faithfully changed the classroom bulletin borders at every holiday. . . . If only we fit into the jeans we could wear 20 years ago. But would life really be that much better? A simple black border is actually better for many children when it comes to learning; it's less visual noise than a border that changes all the time. And Glenn Close has had an amazing career, no matter the size of her jeans.

Decluttering our classrooms late in the year is ultimately freeing, because it's sometimes about accepting who we are as teachers, colleagues, and learners—not who we think we should be. Filling the trash bags is a small step in letting go of some of those unrealistic notions of what it means to be a good educator.

Judging Books by Their Covers

In his memoir *Surely You're Joking, Mr. Feynman!*, the late Nobel Prize–winning physicist Richard Feynman shares the experience of being on a science textbook review committee for the state of California. The long, funny story is mostly about the absurdity of what lands in science textbooks. But there is one passage that is telling for literacy leaders trying to set priorities.

Feynman recounts how one of the textbooks for review was sent with all blank pages inside. The cover was complete, and inside was a note from the publisher explaining that this was the last in a series they were submitting for review, and that it hadn't been finished in time to meet the committee deadline. The publisher still hoped the other books in the series would be considered, and the blank book was sent to illustrate what the complete set would eventually look like.

Feynman dutifully trouped to the committee meeting with his notes on each textbook, where the group shared rubrics and ratings. Imagine his surprise when the blank book received a rating from six of the ten committee members; some of the committee members had even ranked it higher than complete texts.

The raters were embarrassed, and finally admitted they weren't reading the books. Because they were busy, they were relying on the blurbs from publishers (or even the authors' reputations) instead of taking the time to actually read the books they were recommending. Feynman puzzled through the strange experience and came to this conclusion:

> *I believe the reason for all this is that the system works this way:*
> *When you give books all over the place to people, they're busy;*
> *they're careless; they think, "Well, a lot of people are reading this*
> *book, so it doesn't make any difference . . ."*

(295)

Reading these words, I'd like to believe that I would have been like Dick Feynman on that committee, carefully reading every textbook, taking notes, and having my thorough work be an example to my peers. But when I've been too busy professionally and taken on too much, I'm afraid that at times I've been more like one of those committee members who cut corners and did a mediocre or substandard job.

Here's the thing: every single member of that committee was a leader, a top scientist or educator or policy maker. The problem wasn't that they didn't have the skills to do the job. The problem was they took on too much, and then found themselves becoming sloppy and careless.

The lesson for you as a literacy leader? You have to learn to say no more often. If you are friendly, competent, and dependable, you'll be asked by colleagues to do far more than you can possibly accomplish this year. Each task taken individually is something you can complete well. Too many tasks, and none are done in a way that reflects your true ability. There is nothing more discouraging when you're confident and capable than finding yourself rushing through work and doing a sloppy or haphazard job.

Reference

Feynman, Richard. 1997. *Surely You're Joking, Mr. Feynman!* New York: W. W. Norton.

The Fred Factor

Our daughter graduated from the wonderful K–8 school in our town. Of all the things we miss from that school community, we may miss Debbie the most. Debbie is the administrative assistant in the front office, and she never fails to greet every child and family member by name. No matter how busy she is, she always has a moment to share a smile or commiserate on the joys and challenge of raising kids.

The children adore her even more than the parents. It seems like every single one of them has a running inside joke with Debbie, connected to sports or hobbies or recess plans. And when my daughter fell ill and it took me an hour to race from a distant meeting to the school to take her to the doctor, it was Debbie who sat on the bench inside the school door and held her hand while she waited for me to arrive.

When the class read tributes at their graduation ceremony, everyone laughed and nodded in agreement when someone said they were lucky to be in a school where you actually enjoyed being sent to the office, because you'd get to talk with Debbie.

I was thinking of Debbie this week while reading *The Fred Factor* by Mark Sanborn. This thin business leadership book tells the true story of Fred the Postman, the author's almost comically gracious and service-oriented mail carrier. Fred is continually coming up with new ways of bundling, personalizing, and generally making mail delivery a creative art form.

Sanborn notes how much he learns about service and a passion for doing good work through watching Fred, distilling "The Fred Factor" down to four principles. The "Freds" in any organization believe the following:

- Everyone makes a difference.

- Everything is built on relationships.

- You must continually create value for others, and it doesn't have to cost a penny.

- You can reinvent yourself regularly.

Debbie is a "Fred," and I meet Freds in every school I visit. Fred is the janitor scrubbing down the hall carpet in the evening long past the time he is off the clock, simply because he wants the school to look its very best for the parent breakfast in the morning. Fred is the education aide planting a flower bed in front of the building, which is surely not part of her job description.

Truth be told, if you're reading these words, there is a good chance you are a Fred and appreciate the other Freds in our midst, no matter their job title.

Reference

Sanborn, Mark. 2004. *The Fred Factor*. New York: Broadway Business Books.

Embracing the Unexpected

Some years ago, a friend of mine who is a kindergarten teacher told me the story of setting up a dramatic play area in her classroom. She decided the theme of the area for the first month would be a shoe store. The teacher threw herself into preparing the area for the children. She borrowed real foot-measuring tools from a local shoe store, got shelves from another outlet, and even had 20 boxes of old shoes, in a variety of sizes, neatly displayed.

During the first play period, the teacher told students they could do whatever they wanted in the play area. A large group eagerly congregated around the shelves and decided they would throw a pretend birthday party for a friend. They upended the foot-measuring device to use it as a cake stand and began to make greeting cards out of the shoe order forms laid out for their use.

Their teacher gently, and then not so gently, began to nudge them toward other possibilities for the play area, with prompts like, "Gee, look at all these shoes! What else could you do here besides have a birthday party?" The kids blithely ignored her. After the birthday girl blew out the candles on the imaginary cake, each child one by one gave her a present to open. Not surprisingly, every present turned out to be a box of old shoes.

Sometimes our best-laid plans have surprising results, no matter the age of the learners in our care. What was your most unexpected result of a well-planned activity this year? How did it change your teaching or work with colleagues?

Learning from Mistakes

> Every great mistake has a halfway moment, a split second when it can
> be recalled and perhaps remedied.
>
> **Pearl S. Buck**

I've been reading the book *Why We Make Mistakes* by Joseph Hallinan. The text has my all-time favorite subtitle: *How We Look Without Seeing, Forget Things in Seconds, and Are All Pretty Sure We Are Way Above Average.* That subtitle neatly summarizes the root cause of all problems in my life.

Anyway, in the book Hallinan shares the remarkable story of how anesthesiologists cut their fatality rates fortyfold more than two decades ago. Ponder that statistic for a moment. It's not 40 percent, *but 40 times*—from one death every 5,000 patients to the current death rate of one every 200,000–300,000 cases.

Through a comprehensive review of procedures, anesthesiologists made three changes that dropped death rates so dramatically. The first change was the simplest. There were two models of machines used to deliver gas to patients. Although the machines had a similar appearance and function, one had controls that turned clockwise, and the other turned counterclockwise. You would think the profession would have caught such an obvious source of errors sooner. Once both machines were designed to have controls move in the same direction, the error rate dropped significantly.

The other changes took more time. Short checklists were developed, similar to what pilots use before taking off. The checklists included every important step in pre-operation procedures, and doctors were required to use them. Finally, the most humbling change for the anesthesiologists may have been the most crucial one: everyone in the room was encouraged to speak up if they saw anything amiss. Doctors aren't necessarily accustomed to being challenged by nurses.

What are the lessons here for literacy leaders? We often lump teachers together as one group when we think about their needs, or we consider each teacher as unique. When it comes to what isn't working with professional development, maybe there is a third way to categorize teachers when thinking through logistics. We're often dealing with two different educator "models" because of generational shifts. There is a large group of late-career teachers, the baby boomers, who may have empty nests and often thrive in the early morning. There is another large group, of early-career teachers, who are just the opposite. They may have babies or young children at home, and because of this may be chronically sleep-deprived.

How is your school adjusting its professional development offerings to meet the needs of these two different groups? For example, Jennifer Allen in Waterville, Maine, always offers at least one or two early morning study groups. The empty nesters love meeting at 7 AM (even on a Monday!) because that is prime time for their energy levels. Early-career teachers usually prefer after-school study groups that end promptly at 4 PM, so that they can pick up their children on time from day care.

When I read about the checklists used by the doctors, I thought about the raging debates over which protocols are best for meetings and professional learning communities. Perhaps the agenda or format isn't nearly as important as simply having one, as well as a timekeeper at each meeting to make sure the group hits every item on the list. A checklist or protocol that doesn't vary much from meeting to meeting also ensures that when the facilitator has to miss a gathering, the group still moves forward with clear expectations.

Finally, when was the last time you asked for input from your students or colleagues about something that isn't going well? Is there time set aside regularly to discuss and reassess plans, checklists, and protocols openly?

What Bruce Springsteen Taught Me About Literacy Leadership

This spring as our Choice Literacy video crew prepared for the last leg of our April and May classroom taping blitz, we discovered that Bruce Springsteen and the E Street Band would be playing at an arena just a few miles from a school in California where we would be taping. We're all huge fans, so I decided concert tickets for the crew would be the perfect gift to celebrate the end of another great year of video production.

Of course, there was a big problem with my plan: any of you who have bought tickets for Springsteen know you can't contact Ticketmaster a few days before a concert and score decent seats. His rabid fans know the moment each concert's seats go on sale months in advance, and are at the computer or phone ready to order. It's not uncommon for all good seats to be gone within an hour of tickets being released. On any given Springsteen Saturday sale day, you can find middle-aged men weeping at their keyboards because they overslept and their home arena is sold out by the time they log in to Ticketmaster. Sure enough, when we checked, the only tickets available for the concert we wanted were singles with obstructed views.

But we were determined, so the crew went to work. Three of us spent time the weekend before the trip scouring the Web, trying to find tips on fan message boards for getting last-minute seats. We discovered a Web group with a long history of fans selling seats at face value only, with controls in place to ensure you could have confidence when purchasing. We knew buying seats from these fans would be an option, though they likely wouldn't be together and it would be a bit of a hassle to pick them up or get them delivered in time.

In browsing at another fan site, we found another hot tip: Ticketmaster had released some prime seats for our concert just days before. Those seats sold out instantly, but rumors were that more would be released over the weekend. We set up a schedule for crew members to check in at Ticketmaster throughout the weekend for new seats. Within 12 hours, a couple hundred seats were released on our watch, and we were able to purchase excellent tickets just a few days before the concert.

So what does this have to do with literacy leadership? Absolutely nothing, except that the principles we used in getting the tickets could be applied to many situations literacy leaders find ourselves in when we're working with colleagues in schools.

When faced with a challenge, instead of starting out on the path well traveled, it's best to go first to the "rabid fan" experts who may have creative alternatives. Whether your goal is improving the children's literature collection at your school or integrating more word work into your literacy program, there is probably a teacher in the school or a group on the Web that can save you research time and dollars. When the topic is their passion, they are more than happy to share their knowledge and save you hours of legwork and hassle. The Bruce fans on the Web were willing to sell their extra tickets at face value or provide insider information on late releases of seats, just for the joy of sharing a fantastic concert with others. If we hadn't gone to the rabid fans for advice, we would have found ourselves sitting behind concrete pillars or spending a fortune buying from scalpers. So often we settle for far less than what we want in schools, or pay more than we can afford for a quick-fix program or outside consultant, because we don't look first to the free or low-cost expertise available in our schools or on the Web.

Don't provide all your new resources at once to colleagues; dole them out throughout the year. Ticketmaster has learned that they can goose their traffic by holding back small numbers of prime seats to popular concerts. By releasing them at unexpected, random times, they keep fans coming back again and again to their site (and likely sell many tickets to other events in the process). When you save part of your budget for gifts of new children's and young adult books for colleagues at study groups and staff meetings throughout the year, or Post-it supplies, or book baskets for library reorganizations midyear as needs arise, you delight your colleagues just when the year is becoming a slog or they need a little pick-me-up. You also reap the rewards of a small surge in enthusiasm for trying something new, just because the materials needed for the change are provided on the spot. Never knowing what treats await them at study groups and staff meetings builds morale in surprising ways throughout the year.

Divide and conquer: our time is short, and our strengths vary.

Literacy leaders, and especially literacy coaches and specialists, are expected to wear many hats as we work with colleagues. We are the professional development coordinators, assessment data analyzers, schedulers, curriculum creators. . . . The list of demands on our time grows and grows. Any one person has terrific skills in some realms and struggles in others. I've noticed that some literacy coaches and specialists who work together in districts are beginning to divide responsibilities among their team to capitalize on strengths. For example, someone who loves poring over data has the title "assessment data coordinator" as part of her literacy coaching position. Another literacy specialist who enjoys organizing meetings is the "professional development event coordinator." If you consider the strengths among your team, and parcel out responsibilities accordingly, work is completed more efficiently, and tasks are done by those who enjoy them the most. Without a team of us working on the ticket issue from different angles, we never would have gotten fine seats so late in the game.

And what an amazing concert it was! May we all be so enthusiastic and at the top of our game professionally as Bruce is, more than 40 years after he first picked up a guitar.

Listen Up

A friend of mine had a problem. She was a principal at a small school ready to hire a new teacher. The hiring committee sent two names to her, each candidate fully qualified for the position. The committee asked her to choose, since the candidates had different strengths that were equally valuable and needed on staff.

Unable to choose, my friend went to the district superintendent. "I'm not asking you to choose," she told him. "I want you to listen first and then ask me good questions until I can figure out what the right choice is." And ask good questions he did:

What is appealing about candidate X?

What is the best work experience candidate Y would bring to the job?

And on and on. As he listened to my friend's response to a question, the next question would emerge naturally.

Finally, after about 30 minutes of questions and listening, he asked one that provided the breakthrough insight: "At some point you and the teacher you hire will disagree about her teaching practice. When you imagine discussing a disagreement about curriculum, which teacher will be more receptive to talking through your differences?" One of the candidates most definitely seemed more open to criticism, and at that moment, the principal knew whom she would be hiring.

Literacy leaders are expected to have all the answers. I find I often lack the discipline not to blurt out solutions to the problems brought to me by friends as soon as they pop into my head. This may be the biggest paradox of the job: if we want colleagues to trust us with their struggles, it may be best to do more listening and less problem solving when they bring those troubles to us.

I remember years ago I was on a hiring committee, and we were interviewing a top candidate for a faculty position. Her weakness was her youth. If she was offered the job, she would be the least experienced on a team of administrators, often dealing with people who were much more seasoned. One of the members of the hiring committee asked her, "What will you do when someone brings you a problem and you have absolutely no real-world experience in dealing with it? How can you help them?"

Her response: "I've found when people bring a problem to you, they don't usually want an immediate solution. What they want is a sense that you are willing to listen deeply—to acknowledge what they are struggling with and then take the time to understand the issue from all angles. From that starting point, you'll have trust, and then you can work through solutions together." With that answer, she got the job.

Rachel Remen writes about listening in *Kitchen Table Wisdom*:

> *I suspect that the most basic and powerful way to connect with another human being is to listen. Just listen. Perhaps the most important thing we ever give to each other is our attention. And especially if it's given from the heart. When people are talking, there's no need to do anything but receive them. Just take them in. Listen to what they are saying. Care about it. Most times caring about it is even more important than understanding it.*

(143)

Learning to listen, and asking questions that show empathy and concern, probably are more important skills for a literacy leader than mastering any research base. You're presented with unique concerns from teacher after teacher, day after day in schools. The more you listen, the more likely teachers will be willing to share their professional failures and frailties with you over time. And if you're not getting the help you need with your professional struggles, don't be shy about asking your trusted colleagues to listen up, question, and keep the solutions to themselves for a while.

Reference

Remen, Rachel. 2006. *Kitchen Table Wisdom.* New York: Riverhead Books.

Dreams and Memories

Recently my family had dinner in a little Mexican cantina, and I was fascinated by the many *dichos* covering the walls. Dichos are proverbs, or pithy cultural truths. This one caught my eye:

> *Cuando joven, de ilusiones; cuando viejo, de recuerdos.*
>
> [For the young, dreams; for the old, memories.]

Here's a simple test to see if you're burning out on the job. Are your happiest thoughts of work dreams of the future, or memories of good times from the past?